THE LEGACY OF ROME

SCOTLAND'S ROMAN REMAINS

THE LEGACY OF ROME

SCOTLAND'S ROMAN REMAINS

LAWRENCE KEPPIE

JOHN DONALD PUBLISHERS
EDINBURGH

This edition published by John Donald Publishers
An imprint of Birlinn Ltd
West Newington House
10 Newington Road
Edinburgh
EH9 1QS

www.birlinn.co.uk

First published 1986
Revised reprint 1990
Second edition 1998
Third edition 2004

ISBN 0 85976 599 7

British Library Cataloguing-in-Publication Data
A catalogue record for this book is available
from the British Library

Typesetting and origination by Brinnoven, Livingston
Printed and bound by GraphyCems, Spain

CONTENTS

PREFACE

This handbook was initially commisioned as an early member of a projected series of guides to aspects of Scottish Archaeology, under the auspices of CBAScotland, now the Council for Scottish Archaeology (CSA), and I remain grateful to Mrs Edwina Proudfoot, then President of CBA Scotland, for inviting me to compile it. A preface by Mrs Proudfoot (1984), augmented by a postscript (1998) by Dr Shannon Fraser, then Director of CSA, ornamented earlier editions.

The success of the handbook (published 1984 by John Donald Publishers) led to a corrected reprint in 1990, and a more thoroughly revised second edition in 1998. Continuing demand has prompted this reformatted and enlarged new (third) edition which takes into account developments and discoveries of recent years. In what follows, Part 1 (The Romans in Scotland) has been revised, but remains of similar length; Part 2 (Visiting Scotland's Roman Remains) has been expanded and a number of fresh illustrations added; more emphasis too is placed on the tribal society into which the Romans intruded in the early centuries AD, though it remains as ever difficult to demonstrate that Iron Age sites were in fact contemporary with the Roman period, or phases of it.

All but a very few sites where something remains visible at ground level were revisited by the author in Spring 2004, or access to them checked. It comes as some relief that many field monuments seem hardly to have deteriorated at all in the last 20 years. Small-scale damage however continues, even at rural sites. Skilful negotiation by Historic Scotland and other bodies can mitigate the impact of development or farming activity. Some recently found sites have been lucky to survive at all to the present day – here I think of the fortlet observed by aerial reconnaissance in 1992 within the new town of Livingston, West Lothian; others must have been lost without record as towns and hamlets have expanded. A cine-film by the late Anne S. Robertson showing the Antonine Wall in 1956–58 has been supplemented by a video record made by the present writer in 2002; similar visual records made at other sites at known dates could be similarly useful.

Currently the Antonine Wall is being proposed as a 'World Heritage Site' in a multinational bid encompassing Roman frontiers in Europe from the Atlantic to the Black Sea. If successfully achieved, WHS status could attract EU funding, encourage local initiatives, prompt international research projects and strengthen the hand of planning authorities.

As ever the author will be grateful for information from readers on alterations to access. Streets can be renamed, roads renumbered, fresh obstacles encountered, fences removed or barriers rendered impenetrable, a never-ending process which will inevitably continue. An extreme example, noted in the second edition, was the complete and expert removal of a disused railway viaduct across the Tarras Water at Broomholm in Dumfriesshire, leaving the intending visitor using the first edition of this book confronted by a fast-flowing river and no apparent means of crossing it. In 1998 I also referred to uncertainty over means of access to the fortlet at Redshaw Burn, South Lanarkshire, where the traditional route had been severed by the M74 motorway, then under construction (see now below, p. 89)

The bibliography has been updated. The line-illustrations have in many cases been enhanced and updated with the aid of computer-based technology. A number of new or replacement photographs have been incorporated.

The author, and many readers too, are now able to access an ever-growing body of online resources, not only to establish the location of sites and learn of their history, but also to view digitised images of the remains, in particular via the CANMORE and CANMAP databases hosted by the Royal Commission on the Ancient and Historical Monuments of Scotland (RCAHMS), and the Scottish Cultural Resources Access Network (SCRAN) database, which at the time of writing holds upwards of 300,000 images taken from museums, galleries and archives. Some relevant websites are listed at p. 192. A selection of artefacts from an increasing number of national, local authority, university and private museums can be viewed online, and their opening hours checked.

The present guide stands in a long tradition: readers may recall the two monographs by Jessie Mothersole (*Agricola's Road into Scotland* and *In Roman Scotland*, both published in 1927), delightfully illustrated by her own sketches and watercolours. In 1960 Professor Anne Robertson's excellent handbook to *The Antonine Wall* was published by the Glasgow Archaeological Society, and has been several times reprinted and revised.

ACKNOWLEDGEMENTS

Many friends and colleagues have over the years responded generously to my requests for information and illustrative materials (see pp. vii–ix of the second edition). I am especially grateful, as ever, to James Walker and Margaret Robb, who have shared with me the pleasure and effort of locating and visiting many of the sites described below, and of looking at them with fresh eyes. For additional information incorporated in the revised text (2004) I am grateful to Professor David Breeze and Ms Andrea Smith (Historic Scotland), Mr Geoff Bailey (Falkirk Museum), Dr David Woolliscroft and Dr Birgitta Hoffmann (University of Liverpool), Mr Donald Gordon and Dr Bill Lonie (Trimontium Trust), Rebecca Jones (RCAHMS), Fraser Hunter (NMS), John Gooder and Murray Cook (AOC Scotland), Edward Powell (Innerpeffray Library), John Richardson (Antonine Guard), Susan Bryson and Ken Fawell. My colleagues at the Hunterian Museum have, as always, offered their support, and I should especially like to thank Jim Devine, Norman Arnold, Iona Shepherd and their colleagues in its Multimedia Studio.

Permission to reproduce photographs was initially given by the Ministry of Defence, BBC Scotland, the Committee for Aerial Photography (University of Cambridge), the Royal Commission on the Ancient and Historical Monuments of Scotland, the Hunterian Museum of the University of Glasgow (and the Hunter Coin Cabinet), the National Museums of Scotland and Falkirk Museum. The late Dr A.A.R. Henderson, Sandy Sharp and Dr Colin Martin generously allowed me to use photographs from their own collections; Professor W.S. Hanson allowed me to reproduce here a view of his excavations at Elginhaugh. I am particularly grateful, as before, to Trevor Graham and his colleagues of the Media Services Unit, University of Glasgow, for their help in preparing many of the photographs for publication. Line illustrations were prepared by the author unless otherwise credited in the captions.

The Roman Scotland Archive at the Hunterian Museum, the compilation of which, based on copies of Ordnance Survey record cards of Roman sites, was initially made possible in the 1980s under a scheme financed by the Manpower Services Commission, has proved an invaluable aid towards the preparation of the 'itineraries' and of the Bibliography. It has been kept up to date through the efforts of Elizabeth Bell. Recently details of its contents have been entered on a database, principally through the efforts of James Lafferty-Furphy, who was awarded a Hunterian Scholarship in 2002 for this purpose. The intention is to make this information available on the Hunterian Museum website in due course.

Lawrence Keppie, Glasgow, June 2004

The Cramond lioness (National Museums of Scotland).

INTRODUCTION

When the Romans first came to Britain in AD 43, in the reign of the emperor Claudius, it may be doubted whether they had any clear intention of advancing as far north as Scotland. However, early successes in overrunning southern England drew Roman armies forward first into northern England and then, in the years after AD 79, into Scotland.

The Romans remained in Scotland, on and off, for at least a century and a half, and exercised some considerable influence over events there for rather longer. Yet even today it is a commonly held belief that Hadrian's Wall, that stupendous monument to Roman power on the crags between Tyne and Solway, was the northern limit to the Roman domain in Britain. This view is widely held both in Scotland – where it testifies to the unconquerable spirit of the indigenous peoples against an invader – and in England where everything north of Hadrian's Wall is considered to have been beyond the Roman pale.

Scotland can boast of no Roman towns or villas, so common in areas further to the South. In general the archaeological remains to be discussed here are the remnants of military installations, built more often in timber and turf than in mortared stonework.

The following pages also contain a brief description of the categories of small finds – inscribed stones and altars, coins, brooches, cooking pots, even shoes and belt buckles – which were lost, left behind or discarded by the army of occupation, and serve to provide us with a fascinating picture of life in the frontier area of Rome's northernmost province. Museums where relics of the Roman presence in Scotland can be viewed are listed below in an Appendix (p. 189).

The handbook is designed to appeal to the reader with little or no prior knowledge of things Roman, yet who wishes to learn something about a brief but action-packed interlude in Scotland's past, when the northern part of the island of Britain became a part of the very extensive Roman Empire. It aims also to provide an impression of how our picture of the Roman period is built up from the literary accounts and the archaeological evidence, so that the reader may see

The Legacy of Rome

what can be legitimately inferred and what must remain, inevitably, hidden from the modern enquirer.

If this handbook achieves anything, it will be to encourage the reader to go out and locate the remains for him- or herself, and visualise their appearance nearly 2000 years ago. The itineraries (pp. 77ff) aim to provide an indication of what may be seen at individual sites, set against the backcloth of Scotland's often spectacular scenery. There is the further hope that this guidebook will help the reader to be able to recognise sites as being Roman, to perceive what distinguishes them from monuments of earlier or more recent epochs, even where no archaeological excavation has ever taken place.

In the following pages two liberties are taken with the name Scotland: firstly that it is used at all, when the reader will remember that the Scots from whom the northern half of the island of Britain takes its present name are not attested historically before the mid-fourth century; secondly that the term will be employed on occasion to encompass all the territory between Shetland and the River Tyne – that is, Scotland can be everything north of Carlisle and Newcastle, and so includes great parts of present-day Northumbria and a little of Cumbria. The Romans knew of no Anglo–Scottish Border on the present line; whenever they moved northwards, their starting point was the Tyne–Solway isthmus.

Key to the Maps

■	fort
▪	fortlet
●	watch-tower
□	camp
— · —	road (course certain)
– – –	road (course probable)
__/__	milestone

land over 250 m (800 ft) stippled

Note the abbreviations RCAHMS = Royal Commission on the Ancient and Historical Monuments of Scotland; HS = Historic Scotland; FC = Falkirk Council.

PART ONE

THE ROMANS IN SCOTLAND

1
SCOTLAND ON THE EVE OF
THE ROMAN INVASION

It has been prevalent in some circles to suppose that when the Romans arrived in Scotland, no one else lived there, or that everyone else promptly left. In fact Scotland had been occupied by humans for over 6000 years since the retreat of the ice sheets had drawn hunters and fishermen to eke out a scanty living in these northern climes. By the mid-first century AD the tribes of Scotland

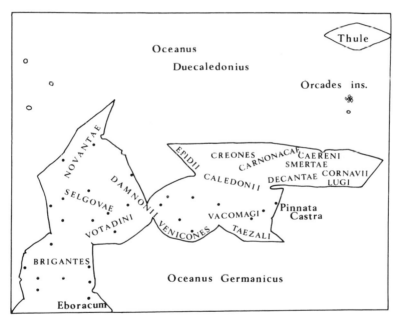

1. **Ptolemy's Map,** compiled *c.*AD 140, showing the major tribes. Much of the information about the interior of Scotland must derive from data collected by Agricola's army in AD 79–83. It is not known why Scotland 'leans over' to the right. Note: The *Orcades Insulae* are the Orkneys; *Thule* is Shetland (or perhaps Iceland). Dots represent places individually named by Ptolemy. *Eboracum* = York. *Pinnata Castra* is a site somewhere on the Moray Firth. See also p. 188.

were making use of iron tools and weapons, and had long since begun
the sowing and harvesting of crops. In Scotland this so-called Iron
Age and the Roman period are contemporary – or more precisely the
Roman invasions amounted to a mere interlude (or even a hiccup) in
the Scottish Iron Age.

Scotland was not a unified country when the Romans invaded,
but was divided into territories occupied by many independent tribes.
Roman geographical writers and compilers give a useful, if often
confusing and enigmatic, digest of knowledge at various times during
the period. The geographer Ptolemy, who compiled a world map
about AD 140, provides a useful picture of the tribes and the areas
they controlled (Fig. 1), but it has never been possible to establish
their boundaries archaeologically. Certainly the Novantae occupied
south-west Scotland, the Selgovae held an upland area further east
centred on the upper valley of the Tweed, and the Votadini controlled
a wide area of the Lothians between the Forth and the Tweed. The
Damnonii belonged in Ayrshire and the central Lowlands. Beyond
them were the Venicones of Fife, the Vacomagi round the coastline
of NE Scotland, and numerous smaller tribes. For the Romans all
the land north of the Forth–Clyde line was known as Caledonia,
a zone of mountains and trackless forests seemingly inhabited by
wild, naked savages untouched by civilisation. Ptolemy also provides
a list of coastal features and a number of individual placenames,
at least some of which are likely to be identifiable as Roman forts
(below, pp. 00,00,00); of the latter, only *Trimontium* can be located
with anything approaching confidence (below, p. 113). The so-
called Antonine Itinerary lists placenames and distances between
them for the early third century province; only one place within
the boundaries of modern Scotland is named: *Blatobulgium*, that
is Birrens in Dumfriesshire (below, p. 81). The much later Ravenna
Cosmography draws on a variety of sources, and includes a list of
places on or near the long abandoned Antonine Wall, of which one,
Velunia, can be identified as Carriden (below, p. 132).

Essentially this was a warlike society of Celtic peoples, owing
allegiance to local chieftains. Archaeology shows a wide variety of
settlement-types in use in Scotland at this time: circular stone-built
or timber houses in central and southern Scotland, together with
crannogs (lochside hutments often raised out of the water on wooden
piles), souterrains (stone-walled underground stores associated with
circular huts at ground level), duns (low circular stone towers) and

brochs (lofty stone towers). There were no towns. As centres of population, or at least centres of defence, we can see the hillforts which abound in most areas, though a great many were probably long abandoned.

2
THE ROMANS IN SCOTLAND: AN HISTORICAL OUTLINE

The Romans first came to Britain in 55 BC when Julius Caesar and his legions landed on a beach near Dover. Caesar's exploits in Britain in 55 (and in greater strength in 54) were shortlived, even though he claimed the total subjection of Britain to impress public opinion at Rome (Fig. 2). Almost exactly a century later, in AD 43, the emperor Claudius mounted a full-scale invasion of Britain, and his forces quickly overran the south-eastern corner of the island. Progress thereafter was slow, and the province was all but lost to Rome in AD 60–61 with the outbreak of a major rebellion under Boudica – the Boadicea of legend. A civil war in AD 68–69 brought to power the emperor Vespasian and a new dynasty, the Flavians, who initiated a forward movement in Britain: the governor Q. Petillius Cerealis overran northern England, to the Tyne–Solway line, if not further; his successor Sex. Julius Frontinus subdued the Silures of south Wales. The way was thus clear for a major assault on the northern half of the island. The governor fated to direct the campaigns into Scotland was Gnaeus Julius Agricola, a safe and uninspiring supporter of the Flavian dynasty, who had twice before seen service in Britain.

Agricola's campaigns

Our appreciation of Agricola's activities is immeasurably enriched by the survival to modern times of an account of his life written just a few years after his death by his son-in-law, the distinguished Roman historian Cornelius Tacitus. This marriage connection effectively secured Agricola's posthumous fame, and has given us a detailed account of and chronological framework for his campaigns in northern Britain. Without it we should not know exactly when the Romans first penetrated into Scotland, how many seasons the army campaigned there, and what the outcome was.

Agricola arrived in Britain as legate (governor) in the late summer of AD 77 (the date now preferred by most scholars; the alternative is AD 78) and undertook a lightning campaign in north Wales, which

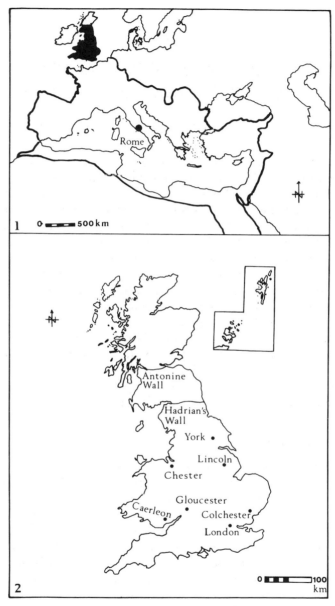

2. Above: **The Roman Empire,** *c.* AD 140, during the reign of Antoninus Pius.
Below: **Roman Britain,** *c.* AD 140, showing some of the chief towns, military
bases and the two frontier walls.

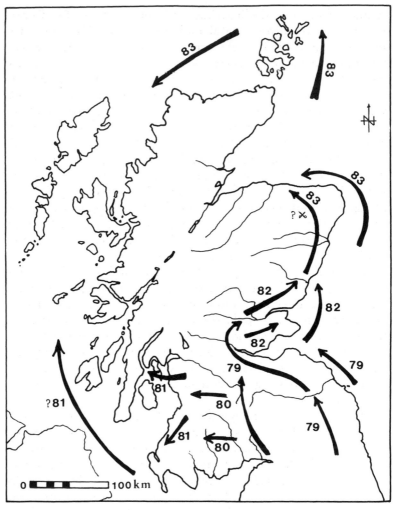

3. **Agricola's campaigns by land and sea, AD 79–83,** which culminated in a battle at *Mons Graupius.*

put an end to resistance there. In the following year he consolidated Roman control over northern England.

By the early summer of AD 79 he was ready to move further north (Fig. 3). Assembling a substantial battle-group which must have numbered some 20,000 men (based on the four legions available, together with auxiliary troops; see below, p. 21), he advanced through southern Scotland to the line of the Forth and then to the Tay. Tacitus does not report any meaningful resistance from the tribes, but notes that bad weather hindered the army's advance. In the following year (AD 80, which Agricola could reasonably have supposed would be his last in Britain – governors normally served for about three years on a single posting), he concentrated his efforts on consolidation work within areas already overrun and on the placing of garrisons along the outer limits of the newly enlarged province. In particular he established forts in the valley between Forth and Clyde, which he saw would make a suitable northern frontier line. However, in Rome it seems likely that the new Emperor Titus, who had succeeded his father Vespasian in AD 79), was sufficiently impressed by the ease of Agricola's advance to extend his appointment (probably for a further three-year period), with instructions to continue. How far the emperor appreciated the nature of the terrain that Agricola's army would now have to face is unknown to us.

In the spring of AD 81 Agricola turned again to his task, beginning an investigation of land routes up the west coast, taking part in at least one sea-crossing, perhaps into Argyllshire. In the same summer he despatched some ships up the west coast. He also placed garrisons on the coast facing Ireland and allegedly pondered an expedition there. However, there is no reliable evidence that the Romans ever invaded Ireland, or established any temporary or permanent installations there, though Roman goods were undoubtedly traded to the island in some quantity.

One summer was enough to show Agricola that the best way northwards in Britain was not up the west coast, with its almost continuous belts of mountains and sea lochs. In AD 82 he turned his attention to the east coast and moved forward from the Tay into Strathmore, on the traditional route followed by invaders from the South. But the tribes proved an elusive quarry, adept all the while at falling upon his extended communication lines, and he suffered a scare when the Caledonians assaulted one of his task-forces; they were beaten off only with some difficulty.

In the following year (AD 83) events moved towards a climax. Agricola must have known that his own term of office could not be much more prolonged. Equally the emperor in Rome, Domitian (who had succeeded Titus in September AD 81), with his mind on campaigns in Germany, may well have encouraged Agricola to bring the British war to a prompt and suitable close, with fanfares to indicate an

acceptable victory. Tacitus tells us nothing about the movements of
Agricola's forces in the spring and early summer of AD 83. We could
suppose that no engagement was fought; certainly none was won. As
to the whereabouts of the army, archaeology indicates that in AD 82
or 83 (or in the course of both summers) Agricola had succeeded in
moving forward past the Grampian mountains into the flatter country
of Moray and Nairn, where he is believed to have reached the valley
of the Spey and may easily have gone further.

By the late summer of AD 83, with the Caledonians as elusive
as ever, and Agricola's own time running out, word came of a
concentration of Caledonian warriors, some 30,000 in all, under a war-
leader, Calgacus, at a hill which Tacitus names as *Mons Graupius* (the
Graupian Mountain). Agricola advanced quickly to this position, with
a minimum of heavy baggage, to confront the tribesmen before they
repented of a decision to face the Romans in a set-piece encounter.

Agricola formed up his army in traditional Roman fashion, with
auxiliary infantry in the centre and cavalry on each flank. But he held
back his main strength, the legions, as a reserve, and in the event they
were not needed. The Caledonians had a number of war-chariots (a
military vehicle long relegated on the Continent to museums and
ceremonial parades); we are told that Roman cavalry soon dispersed
them. The auxiliaries then advanced up the slopes of *Mons Graupius*
and, just as they seemed likely to be enveloped by the masses of
Caledonians filtering round their flanks down the hillside, Agricola
unleashed a reserve force of 2000 cavalry in flank and rear; victory
was his. Tacitus gives Roman casualties at 360 and Caledonian losses
at about 10,000. After the battle Agricola instructed his fleet to sail
round the north coast of Scotland, from east to west, as though to
emphasise the totality of the conquest.

The location of *Mons Graupius* has never been satisfactorily
established. Tacitus implies that it lay close to, and perhaps even
within sight of, the sea, and far away in the north of Britain. A good
case has been made out for identifying *Mons Graupius* with the great
mass of Bennachie close to Inverurie, near which a large Roman
marching camp was located by aerial photography at Durno in the
later 1970s (Fig. 4; below, p. 186). Another candidate for the site could
be the distinctive peak of Craig Rossie, much further south, near
Dunning in Perth & Kinross (below, p. 169). A mistake made by its
printer in the text of Tacitus' biography of Agricola, when it was set as
a book in the 1470s, led to the spelling *Grampius* instead of *Graupius*;

4. **Mount Bennachie,** perhaps the battle-site of *Mons Graupius,* seen from the marching camp at Durno (Photo: Dr A.A.R. Henderson). See also p. 186.

hence our Grampian Mountains, Grampian Television and the former Grampian Region, all of which should be 'Graupian'!

The battle at *Mons Graupius* formed the climax to Agricola's governorship, and shortly afterwards (with the end of the campaigning season) he was recalled to Rome, and never again commanded an army in the field. Agricola's successor, whose name remains unknown, saw to the establishment of many forts and roads in Scotland, deep into Strathmore (Fig. 5). The kingpin of the system was a fortress for a legion, of some 21.7 ha. (53.5 acres), at Inchtuthil on the Tay (below, p. 178). Construction work there was underway in AD 86. Forts were also placed at the mouths of glens leading in towards the Highlands, and others on lines of communication back to the Tay, the Forth and the southern part of the British province.

With the departure of Agricola a veil is drawn over the history of Scotland for half a century. The modern historian is abruptly thrown back on the archaeological record whose imperfections become all too apparent. The years following AD 85 witnessed a sequence of Roman disasters in her Danubian provinces, involving a serious loss of troops, and the garrison of Britain was cut back to fill the gaps.

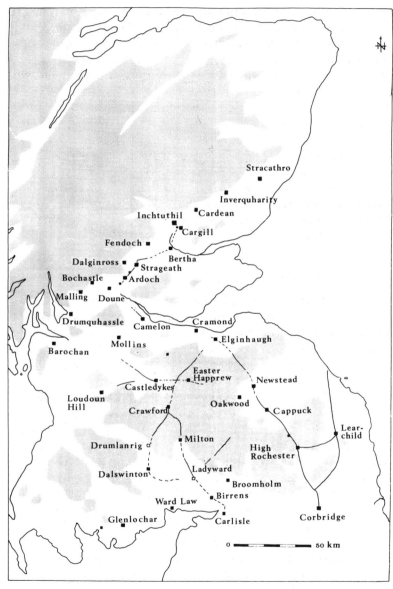

5. **Forts and roads** in Scotland in the Flavian period, AD 80–c. 100. The sites of fortlets are not individually named.

The opportunity was thus lost, if it had ever existed, of completing for Rome the conquest of the entire island. The base at Inchtuthil was abandoned in about AD 87 and with it all the forts north of the Tay. The Roman army fell back, it seems, to the line of the River Earn. Within a few years a further withdrawal had begun, which brought Roman troops back to the Forth–Clyde line, and very shortly to the Cheviots. The archaeological record is insufficiently precise to allow every stage in the withdrawal to be accurately documented. However, by the turn of the century it seems clear that the Roman forces had fallen back to the Tyne–Solway line, along which a cordon of military posts was subsequently established. When in the early 120s AD, under the Emperor Hadrian, a great barrier of stone and turf – Hadrian's Wall – was built along the crags just north of this line, it must have seemed that the Roman interlude in Scotland's past was decisively over.

The Antonine period

In AD 138 Hadrian was succeeded by Antoninus Pius, whose accession had an immediate effect on the frontier in Britain. The army was ordered to move forward again and to begin construction of a new frontier line, this time in central Scotland – the Antonine Wall. A biography of Antoninus, written nearly two centuries later, reports that, 'having thrust back the barbarians and having built a second wall, this time of turf, he conquered the Britons through his legate Lollius Urbicus'. This new wall was built in AD 142–143; coins were issued to mark the successful northwards extension of the British province (Fig. 6). We may think that the decision to move forward again was testimony to disturbances and unrest in northern Britain, and even of the failure of the newly completed Hadrian's Wall. More probably, however, the advance has to be linked to Antoninus' need – like that of Claudius a century before – to acquire military prestige; his advisors may have felt that it could be most easily won in Britain, by what in effect was a recovery of lands already overrun and briefly held at the time of Agricola's campaigns half a century before.

The Antonine Wall, built of turf on a substantial stone-built base, stretched for 60 kms (37 miles) between Bo'ness on the Forth and Old Kilpatrick on the Clyde (below, p. 127). Along the line of the Wall were placed fortlets, very probably at every Roman mile, and at wider intervals there were forts, initially perhaps six in all, each

6. **Coin** (*sestertius*) **of Antoninus Pius,** commemorating the reconquest of Scotland, issued AD 143–44. (a) obverse showing head of Antoninus; (b) reverse showing personification of Victory with a laurel wreath, and the legend BRITAN, i.e. *Britannia* (Photos: Hunter Coin Cabinet).

housing a regiment of auxiliaries. The building of the Wall was commemorated by setting up a series of large stone plaques – now known as distance slabs – inscribed with Latin texts giving details of the distances completed by each work-party (below, p. 45; Figs. 7, 28–30, 88). The task was undertaken by men from the three legions of the garrison of Britain. After a year or two, extra forts were added, at much closer intervals.

The Antonine Wall did not exist in isolation. Many forts were built along the main communication routes in southern Scotland, often on sites used by Agricola's troops (Fig. 8). A map or written record must have been kept from the time of the earlier occupation; doubtless ramparts and ditches would still be visible, if overgrown after the passage of half a century. A few forts were also constructed north of the Antonine Wall as far as the mouth of the Tay. It may be that these were intended to close off, or protect, the peninsula of Fife, whose inhabitants (from the archaeological record a culturally distinct grouping) seem thus to have been afforded some protection by Rome.

It used to be a common belief, based on a combination of literary and archaeological evidence, that around AD 155/157 there was trouble

7. **Defeat of the native tribes,** AD 142–43: a scene from the sculptured distance slab found in 1868 at Bridgeness, Falkirk (Photo: National Museums of Scotland).

on the northern frontier line, with many forts – perhaps the entire system – abandoned, only to be rebuilt within a few years. Now it appears more likely that such trouble was localised; if it did cause the Wall to be given up, the interlude was brief. At any rate, soon after the accession in AD 161 of a new emperor, Marcus Aurelius (or at least within the decade AD 160–170), most of the forts in Scotland were demolished or abandoned. The army returned to the line of Hadrian's Wall, whose installations were refurbished to receive them. A few forts were maintained northwards into Dumfriesshire and as

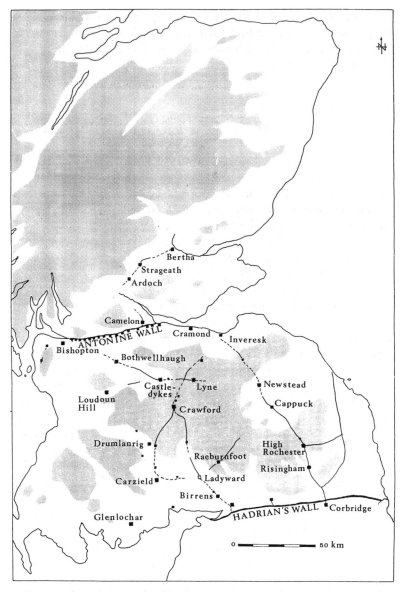

8. **Forts and roads** in Scotland in the Antonine period, AD 142–*c*.AD 165. The sites of fortlets are not individually named.

far as the Tweed until about AD 180, but by that date, or soon after, the garrisons were pulled back further, and Hadrian's Wall with some forward outposts to the Cheviots became effectively the northern frontier of the province.

The expedition of Severus

In general, although specific information is lacking, it seems that the northern frontier in Britain was restive throughout the decades following the Roman withdrawal from Scotland. Finally in AD 208 the then emperor, Septimius Severus, arrived in Britain, accompanied by his sons Caracalla and Geta, together with substantial military forces, to mount a major campaign in the north, specifically against two tribes – named as the Maeatae (perhaps in Stirlingshire and Strathmore), and the Caledonians who lived 'beyond them'. In AD 209 the imperial task-force, perhaps some 40,000 men, crossed the line of Hadrian's Wall and (according to the historian Cassius Dio who wrote soon after) invaded 'Caledonia' (Fig. 9). Very probably a fleet accompanied the army up the east coast. Casualties were heavy, but the advance continued until the emperor arrived 'almost at the end of the island'. A treaty was arranged with the native tribes, now suitably cowed, by which some territory was yielded; Severus and Caracalla both took the title *Britannicus*, 'conqueror of Britain' (Fig. 10). But the celebrations were premature: the next year was marked by a rebellion suppressed, probably by Caracalla, as Severus himself was ill. One reason for revolt may have been the realisation that the Romans intended to remain in Scotland, for construction had very probably already begun on a fortress which could have housed about half a legion at Carpow on the southern side of the Tay at Newburgh; both the Second and the Sixth legions had a part in the building work (below, p. 170). This was a new Inchtuthil – a powerful base close up against the known or likely source of future trouble. Early in AD 211 Severus, worn down by the pressures of an energetic life, died at York. Caracalla succeeded him, with the army's support. The ancient historians tell us that Caracalla left immediately for the continent and Italy, to consolidate his political position, abandoning the Scottish conquests. However, an inscribed stone from Carpow (below, p. 170) may testify to continued building activity within the new reign. But it was not long before the army finally withdrew.

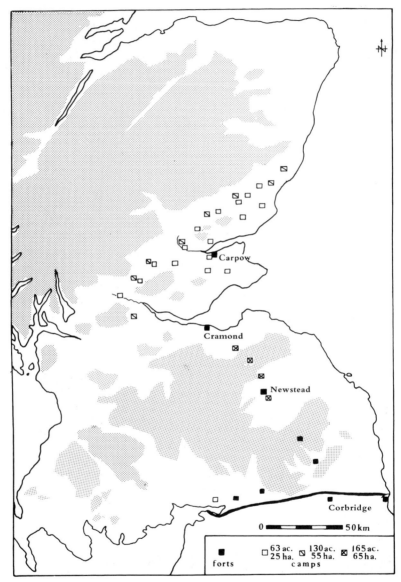

Carpow

Cramond

Newstead

Corbridge

	63 ac.	130 ac.	165 ac.
	25 ha.	55 ha.	65 ha.
forts		camps	

0 _____ 50 km

9. **Campaigns of the emperor Septimius Severus,** AD 208–211, showing marching camps north of Hadrian's Wall, and forts occupied at this time.

Scotland after the Roman Withdrawal

After the departure of Caracalla silence descends on the northern frontier. This may by itself imply that the Severan campaigns had been a success: the northern tribes had taken a severe beating, or enough of a shock to keep the frontier quiet for several generations. But if Scotland as such was abandoned, some permanent forts were maintained to the north of Hadrian's Wall as far as the Cheviots, on a line remarkably close to the modern border between Scotland and England, their garrisons being large all-purpose auxiliary units of mixed infantry and cavalry, which would have had the capacity to range widely, even up to the Forth–Clyde line.

Although the Roman interlude in Scottish history was now effectively over – that is, the attempts to place military forces north of the Cheviots were not repeated – the Romans doubtless continued to try to influence the tribes of the north, seeking alliances, supporting factions in tribal strife, or promising largesse in return for peaceful relations (below, p. 188). Roman patrols, it has been suggested, might still have been seen along the main river valleys beyond the formal frontier line. But from about the AD 290s onwards the Roman province began to suffer devastating raids from the North, and also

10. **Coin (*sestertius*) of Caracalla,** commemorating the Severan campaigns in Scotland, issued AD 211. (a) obverse showing head of Caracalla; (b) reverse showing Victory piling up captured weaponry, with the legend VICT BRIT, i.e. *Victoriae Britannicae*, 'victories won in Britain' (Photos: Hunter Coin Cabinet).

from Ireland and the continent. The Romans were increasingly on the defensive, no longer holding the initiative and dictating terms.

Foremost among the enemies of Roman Britain in the centuries which followed were the Picts (*Picti*) who are first mentioned by a Roman historian in the year AD 297. In AD 306 they were defeated by the Emperor Constantius somewhere in the northern half of Britain, perhaps to the north of Hadrian's Wall, though no secure evidence for his activities has yet been found in Scotland itself. Popular imagination supposes that the Picts were the chief adversaries of the Romans in earlier centuries too, but it seems that they only became powerful towards the end of the third century. Their origin has been much disputed, but the question need not concern us here. Most probably we should think of the name *Picti* (i.e. painted men) as indicating a new power grouping in the north rather than identifying a tribe newly arrived from elsewhere. At any rate the weight and severity of their attacks on Roman Britain increased, and contributed substantially to the decline of the province's prosperity.

By the time the clouds partly lift to reveal the Scotland of the seventh century AD (occupied by Picts in the north and east, the Angles in the south-east, the British kingdom of Strathclyde and the Scots on the west coast), the memory of a Roman occupation must have passed almost completely from the minds of the population, kept alive only in popular legend and by a few scholars until the rediscovery of Latin literature at the Renaissance.

3
THE ROMAN ARMY

The Roman imperial army was the force which overran Scotland and added its more southerly part to the Roman Empire. In a popular (but mistaken) modern view this army consisted of stocky Italians, somewhat darker-skinned than the local tribes. 'They must have found it cold in winter' is a common remark, usually expressed in mixed tones of sympathy and amusement. In truth the Roman army in Scotland contained but few Italians, and almost certainly no one who came from Rome itself.

In the period of Rome's growth from small city-state to the foremost power in Italy, and then of the Mediterranean world, her soldiers had indeed been drawn from her own citizens, for whom the task of fighting on the state's behalf was envisaged as both a duty and a privilege. After the civil wars of the later first century BC, the first Roman emperor, Augustus, introduced reforms which made the army a lifetime's career and its members professional soldiers. Since Italians soon proved unwilling to tolerate the new conditions which required long service in distant provinces, subsequent emperors turned increasingly to the manpower of the provinces themselves. The Roman army ceased to be an army of Romans, but an army defending Rome – a city that few of its soldiers can have visited or were likely to see during the long years of military service. This transition was still in progress when Agricola's legions reached Scotland, but by the reign of Antoninus Pius it can be judged complete. The army had become a cosmopolitan force which resembled in training, tactics and general appearance the force of centuries before, but in actuality the soldiers were loyal to the emperor who paid them, and to the good things that the Empire had brought to their homelands, not to the senate and people of the Roman city. Just as in the Second World War the British army contained many not born in Britain and with few words of English at their disposal on enlistment, so the Roman legions opened their ranks to the tribesmen of the provinces, who were straightaway given Roman names and citizenship and once in uniform could hardly be distinguished from their comrades. Many Roman soldiers must have had only a smattering of Latin when they joined the ranks, to be augmented by the vocabulary of the barrack room and the parade ground.

The Roman army in Britain, which moved north to enter Scotland in the later first century, then again in the mid-second, and briefly again in the early third, consisted of two main elements: legionaries (Fig. 11) and auxiliaries. All were professional soldiers, who joined for 25 years and might be held longer.

The legions were the backbone of the Roman army. Each legion contained some 5000 legionaries, arranged into 10 cohorts of about 480 men; the cohorts themselves were divided into centuries of 80 men and into squads of eight, the basic unit (called a *contubernium*), who shared a tent while the army was on campaign and a barrack room in a permanent fortress. All the legionaries at this time were armed and equipped as heavy infantry, with iron cuirasses, bronze or

11. **Roman legionaries.** Trajan's Column, Rome. (Photo: Hunterian Museum.)

iron helmets, curving rectangular shields which offered substantial protection to the body, a short thrusting sword worn at the right side, and a dagger, as well as one or more throwing javelins. The legionaries were thus equipped both for attack and defence; needless to say they were generally expected to attack. The legion was commanded by its legate (*legatus legionis*), a senator, who held his post for about three years before moving on to another, probably civilian, appointment elsewhere in the Empire.

The legions were supported in battle by regiments of auxiliaries, who were normally stationed in front of the legions on a frontier line, while the latter constituted a strategic reserve. The auxiliaries were organised into *cohortes* (cohorts) of infantry usually of 480 men (on the legionary model – though some regiments were larger, up to 1000 men), and into *alae* (wings) of cavalry, usually about 500 men, though here too some regiments were of a larger size. Sometimes infantry and cavalry were combined in a single regiment, a *cohors equitata*, to increase its mobility and capability. These auxiliaries were non-citizens and would obtain citizenship on completion of their service, 25 years. The regiments took their names from the tribe or city of origin, for example the Sixth Cohort of Nervii (from the Low Countries), the First Cohort of Hamii, from the town of Hama in Roman Syria, and the Second Cohort of Thracians (from Bulgaria), all of which were based for a time on the Antonine Wall in central Scotland.

12. **The Antonine Guard**, on parade at Ardoch (Photo: J. Ferguson). On the left is a Syrian archer, on the right is a legionary centurian.

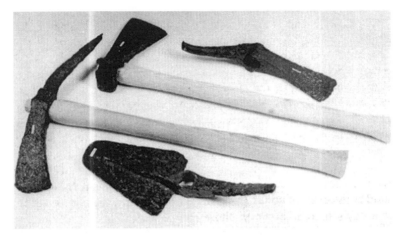

13. **Tools** for ditch-digging and wood-cutting (Photo: Hunterian Museum).

In his biography of Agricola, Tacitus records that a newly enrolled cohort of Usipi (a tribe from the east bank of the Rhine near Frankfurt), formed about AD 80–82 and immediately transferred to Britain for training, where discipline was beaten into them by unsympathetic centurions, was roused to mutiny in the winter of AD 82/83 and killed the officers. Commandeering three small vessels, the unhappy soldiers sailed for home round the north-west coast of Scotland; but few were to survive the hazards of hunger, cannibalism and stormy weather to reach the northern coast of Germany, where the survivors were promptly enslaved by local tribes unsympathetic to their plight.

For a time after initial formation of auxiliary regiments, an attempt was made to keep up recruitment from the original source, but gradually the ranks were filled from whatever manpower was available, usually from local sources within the province where the regiment was stationed. Though the regiments lost their particular ethnic composition, yet the traditions of the homeland, religious beliefs and any distinctive equipment might be retained, especially where regimental tradition required it.

Men from Britain joined the Roman army: already at *Mons Graupius* Agricola had among his army auxiliary regiments recruited in southern Britain. Regiments of auxiliaries formed in Britain, including probably southern Scotland after the conquest, were sent to other provinces: we happen to know of a man from Leicester who enlisted about AD 85 and shared in a moment of glory when his cohort of Britons was decorated in the field, and given citizenship 'before the completion of their due service', by the emperor Trajan during his great war in Dacia (modern Romania) in AD 106.

Agricola's army in the far north of Britain consisted of four legions: II *Augusta* ('Augustan'), II *Adiutrix* ('Supportive'), IX *Hispana* ('Spanish') and the XX *Valeria Victrix* ('Valiant and Victorious'). Soon after the end of Agricola's campaigns in the north, II *Adiutrix* was moved from Britain to the Danube frontier, to reinforce the garrisons there against serious inroads from across the river. Sometime in the period 110–120 legion IX *Hispana* was transferred to Germany, and then (as some think) to the eastern provinces of the Empire. Old theories about the 'disappearance' of the Ninth Legion, and the loss of its eagle-standard, in battle or by desertion in northern Britain, perhaps even in Scotland, have no foundation in the historical record and are now discredited. In about 122 legion VI *Victrix* ('Victorious') arrived in Britain from the Rhineland as a replacement. Thereafter the three legions, II *Augusta*, VI *Victrix* and XX *Valeria Victrix*, formed the permanent legionary garrison of Britain until the later fourth century.

As the army in Britain settled to a routine existence of patrols, manoeuvres and minor skirmishes, in the role of a frontier police, garrisons became more static; a soldier and his regiment might spend 25 years on a single posting. For men below the rank of centurion there was no system of transfers between provinces, to provide a variety of experience, terrain, climate and enemy. A posting to a legion or an auxiliary regiment stationed in Britain probably meant a lifetime in the island. For the garrison of a fort in northern Britain, the centre of the Empire and the city of Rome must have seemed very distant indeed.

4

ROMAN MILITARY INSTALLATIONS

What we see on the ground today in Scotland, or can observe from the air, are the camps, forts, roads and frontier works of the Roman army in what must often have been a hostile countryside. To the indigenous tribes, the installations and the institutions of the armed forces of the Roman Empire must surely have been the cause of much interested observation. The neat square encampments, the trumpet calls, the religious ceremonies, the orderliness and the discipline have impressed countless observers down to modern times.

The military installations of the Roman army comprised temporary or 'marching' camps, forts, fortlets, watch-towers, the fortresses of the legions, and the roads which allowed prompt communication and swift reinforcement of the scattered garrisons. It is time now to consider each category in greater detail.

Temporary camps

Early editions of Ordnance Survey maps designated as Roman camps many upstanding earthworks of diverse period and size, which local pride over the years had ascribed to the Romans, even to Julius Caesar himself, in areas of Britain he cannot conceivably have traversed. Similarly in France *camps de César* proliferated. Sites which we can now see belong in the Iron Age, or which can be identified as medieval, were once confidently designated Roman.

In the pages that follow, the term 'camp' is used for a temporary enclosure, used perhaps only once by a Roman army on the march, and defended by a single narrow ditch and a low mound. A 'fort', on the other hand, is a permanent base in use over many years, and containing timber or stone-built accommodation, where a soldier might spend a considerable part of his military service.

Delimiting an encampment serves to define it, and to discourage straying, and the unannounced or unwelcome arrival in the tent-lines of two or four-legged intruders by night or day. Gradually the Roman camp-layout became standardised, if not fossilised, over the centuries. 'They seem,' said the 4th-century military writer Vegetius, 'to carry a fortified city with them wherever they go.' The end product, certainly, was the throwing up in a brief space of two or three hours of a defended encampment within which each squad of men knew from long training the allotted position where its tent would be pitched.

Camps found in Scotland either by fieldwork or aerial reconnaissance have confirmed that the traditional layout was maintained. Camp defences consisted of a single ditch, usually v-shaped, with the spoil piled on the inner side to form a low rampart topped by palisade-stakes (Figs. 13–15). Within the camp were lines of tents. In the centre of the camp were the larger tents of the commander and his staff.

Excavation of the interior of a camp normally reveals little to the archaeologist – at most some cooking areas or ovens, or refuse pits (but see below, p. 183, for the results of recent excavation at Kintore, Aberdeenshire). In exceptional conditions the general layout of the tents within the camp may be reconstructed – aerial photographs of camps beside the legionary fortress at Inchtuthil show neat lines of refuse pits presumably next to each row of tents. Wooden tent-pegs, strikingly similar to the modern equivalent, have been recovered from several sites, as have some leather tent-panels.

In Scotland many camps have survived impressively as upstanding monuments in rough heathland, better perhaps than in any other part of the Roman Empire. They formed a source of great excitement to the surveyor William Roy when first he had them planned in the 1750s (below, p. 59). Many can still be seen, though in a reduced state, even today. What visitor on the moors above Ardoch cannot be thrilled by the banks and ditches in the heather-covered landscape, as though abandoned by the Romans scarcely a few years ago? Other camps have been discovered only from the air (below, p. 62), their ditches visible in the heat of a summer's drought as a green strip in a field under crop.

There is a great variation in size, between camps for small detachments and those housing large armies. Often camps of similar size are found at intervals of about 24–26 km (15–16 miles), the regular norm for a day's march. Some of those camps which lie in the vicinity of permanent forts may have served to house the fort-builders themselves. More often they must indicate only a task-force in transit which had stopped close to a fort. Small camps in the vicinity of the Antonine Wall (below, p. 131) are likely to have housed work-details engaged on the construction or maintenance of the frontier.

Because of the absence of interior buildings in timber or stone and the shortness of their lifespan, few small finds are generally made during the excavation of a camp. As a result camps may be difficult, or impossible, to date, unless a study of their size, relative proportions or some peculiarity of gate-plan suggests a context for their construction and use.

The progress of a particular task-force across the landscape can be followed by observation of camps of similar size: one group of camps of 65 ha. (165 acres) has been pinpointed in Lauderdale, between the Tweed and the Forth. These camps must have held a substantial part of the army of Roman Britain and could be assigned to the campaigns of the Emperor Septimius Severus in AD 208–211. Other groups of camps in Strathmore, of 25 and 55 ha. (63 and 130 acres), may testify to the movements of smaller forces, perhaps also of the period of Severus (Fig. 9); those of the 25 ha. series regularly have a small annexe attached to one side, perhaps to house a holding garrison when the main army moved on (see Fig. 98).

Attention can also be directed towards camps with a highly unusual ditch system at their gateways, called 'Stracathro-type' camps

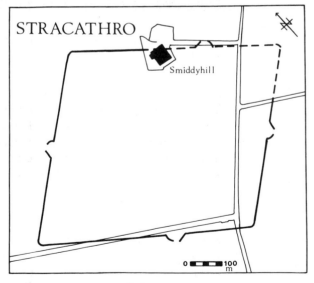

14. **Stracathro, Angus:** ground-plan of a marching camp with distinctive gateways, which can be dated to the Flavian period (after St Joseph). See also Fig. 100.

15. **Dalginross, Perth & Kinross:** aerial view of a marching camp with 'Stracathro' gateways and (to its left) a permanent fort, seen from the SW (Photo: RCAHMS, Crown copyright). See also p. 174.

from the first of the group to be studied in detail, beside the fort of Stracathro in Angus (Fig. 14; see also below, p. 183). At one side of the gate the ditch swings out in a quarter circle (a feature known as a *clavicula*); at the other there is a short section of straight ditch angled at 45 degrees. Such arrangements were designed to make an attack on the gateway more difficult, by restricting access to it. More than a dozen camps with their entrances protected in this way are known in Scotland, and others are suspected. From the location of some 'Stracathro' camps next to forts occupied only in the Flavian period, we can assume that they reflect the movements of Agricola's forces, or those of his immediate successor (Fig. 15). Other camps have their gateways protected by a short length of traverse-rampart and ditch, called a *titulus* (a Latin word meaning 'strip' or 'label'), placed some 10 m in front of the gateway itself and lying parallel to it. Sometimes entrances were of a complexity which only excavation can disentangle.

Precisely how many men could have been accommodated in any camp cannot be known, though estimates have frequently been attempted. A legion of some 5000 men seems likely to have needed a camp of about 12 ha. (30 acres) when on the march; in a permanent fortress it occupied about 20 ha. (50 acres). But we can never be certain of the composition of a task-force, which might comprise both infantry and cavalry, with auxiliaries as well as legionaries housed together in a single camp.

Forts

In the archaeological record, camps and forts can generally be easily distinguished: forts are usually small, up to 4 ha. (10 acres), and are usually defended by two or more ditches, in contrast to a single ditch round a camp; the ramparts and internal buildings of a fort are more substantial. Fort-building as such belonged to a period not of active campaigning but of the consolidation that followed (Fig. 16). The

16. **Legionaries engaged in the building of a turf and timber fort.** Trajan's Column, Rome (Photo: Hunterian Museum).

installations which we term Roman forts were built usually to house individual regiments of auxiliaries, the legions themselves residing in much larger 'fortresses' (see below, p. 35). Essentially the fort provided accommodation and storage for the soldiers' gear and equipment; it was a base for their activities – we should not suppose that soldiers spent all their days within the fort, on the defensive behind ramparts and gates. Rather, the fort was a jumping-off point, a base for wide-ranging activities, so that surveillance was maintained along the valleys, with patrols looking into native villages and strongpoints as required.

It has often been observed that all Roman forts look alike, but it must be stressed at once that no two are identical. Certainly most buildings were constructed to a fairly standard overall design and their relative positions within the fort were hallowed by experience and tradition. A soldier arriving at one of the gates of a fort would know immediately, by the general layout inside, how to find the commanding officer's house, or the hospital or storebuildings, or the headquarters.

In the Flavian period the internal buildings would all have been timber-framed; archaeologically the only trace may be of slots cut into the ground to receive horizontal sleeper-beams or to guide those erecting the principal uprights. In the Antonine period it was normal to build the headquarters building, and usually the granaries and commanding officer's house in stone, or on stone foundations, while the barracks were timber-framed. A number of full-scale reconstructions have been erected, for example (within Britain) of a timber granary at the Lunt, Coventry, and (more recently) of a stone commanding officer's house and a barrack block at South Shields and of a bath-house at Wallsend, in addition to several continental examples.

In the centre of a fort lay the headquarters building (the *principia*), flanked on one side by the commanding officer's house (the *praetorium*) and on the other by granaries and stores, all laid out with their entrances fronting on to the main street of the fort, the *via principalis*. The remainder of the space was taken up by barracks and stables neatly aligned on the buildings of the central group (Fig. 18).

The headquarters block was distinctive in shape: first the visitor would enter a courtyard, perhaps with rooms to either side (sometimes these contained a weapons' store). Beyond the courtyard was a covered hall, running the width of the building; at one end was a dais from

17. **Timber fort-gate,** as constructed for the BBC TV serial 'The Eagle of the Ninth', near Fintry, 1977 (Photo: L. Keppie; reproduced by courtesy of BBC Scotland).

which announcements could be made to an assembled company. At the back, and opening off the covered hall, was a suite of offices, usually five rooms. The central office, whose frontage would be visible from the main door of the building, was the regimental chapel containing its standards and busts or statues of the emperor. Set into the floor there was often a strongroom or at least a timber- or stone-lined strongbox where the regiment's cash and the soldiers' savings were kept. Sentries in the room above protected both the standards and the cash.

The commanding officer's house stood next to the headquarters. The house was laid out to a fairly standard design – rectangular or square in shape, with rooms round four sides looking inwards to a central courtyard. Visitors to Pompeii will recognise the description,

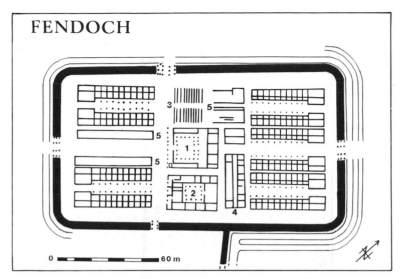

FENDOCH

0 ▬▬▬▬ 60 m

18. **Fendoch, Perth & Kinross:** ground-plan of the Flavian fort (after Richmond). Note: 1 = headquarters, 2 = commanding officer's house, 3 = granaries, 4 — hospital, 5 = stores. The remaining buildings are barracks. See also p. 173.

perhaps more suited to a Mediterranean climate than to northern Britain. Here the commander lived, with ample space for his wife and family, if he chose to expose them to the wild frontier.

If the commanding officer enjoyed space for relaxation and a bearable lifestyle, the soldiers – as in all ages – led the communal life of the cramped barrack room, living and eating in closely confined quarters. The barrack block housed a century of men (i.e. 80 soldiers), in ten compartments – one each for the ten squads (*contubernia*) which made up the century. There was no central cookhouse: each squad cooked as a group, with corn ground down on stone hand-querns and taken for baking to an oven set at the back of the rampart.

On the Scottish frontier, barracks were normally timber-framed with walls of wattles (rather like modern garden fencing) coated with clay. The roofs were of timber slatting, or thatch. The barrack-rooms all had their doors opening on to the same side of the block, where there was often a verandah. At one end of the block, usually that nearer the rampart, was a suite of three or four rooms where the centurion in command had his quarters.

19. **The foundation-trenches for timber-framed barracks,** visible in the sandy subsoil in the upper half of the photograph, under excavation at Elginhaugh, Midlothian, 1986 (Photo: L. Keppie)

The buildings which housed the fort's food supply – usually called 'granaries' – are easily recognised on the ground by their elongated shape, and in the Antonine period by their side-buttresses and solid stone construction. The floors – of laid paving slabs in the stone-built granaries – were raised off the ground on low 'dwarf' walls, allowing the air to pass beneath, through ventilation slots in the side walls. Set into the walls were large, probably louvred windows, and the structure had a heavy overhanging roof. Granaries were thus well designed and expertly built to keep their contents dry and clear of frost and rodents (Fig. 41).

Another important building for the garrison was the bath-house (Fig. 20), which might lie inside the fort up against the rampart, or outside it in an annexe; the bath-house was normally kept away from other buildings to lessen the fire risk from its furnaces. It was always stone-built, and consisted of a sequence of rooms heated to varying temperatures. The bather entered first a cold room, then proceeded through rooms of increasingly higher temperatures, thereafter retracing his steps to the cold room, where water splashed over the body served to close up the pores before the bather dressed and came out again into the open air. Often there was a hot dry 'sauna' room as well. The floors were raised off the ground on a sequence of small

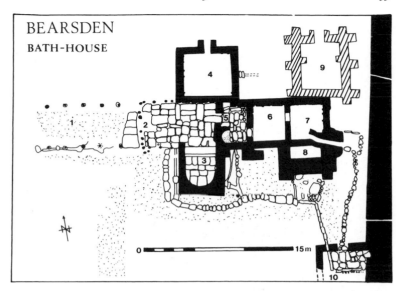

20. **Bearsden on the Antonine Wall:** the fort-bath-house (after Breeze).
Note 1 = changing room, 2 = cold room, 3 = cold plunge bath, 4 = hot dry
room, 5–6 = warm rooms, 7 = hot room, 8 = hot bath, 9 = unfinished heated
room, 10 = latrine. See also p. 151.

pillars or brick stacks (the hypocaust system of underfloor heating),
and heat supplied from one or more furnaces. Heat was also carried
up the walls in sets of square-sectioned clay pipes called box-flues.
A bath-house is always instantly recognisable on excavation, from
the appearance of the hypocausts, or large areas of burning near the
furnaces or from fragments of the orange-red box-flues and hypocaust
bricks, which often survive in vast quantities. The bath-house was
usually quite a small building, and we must suppose a strict rota
for access. The soldiers played games of chance, chatted about their
families and homes, and whiled away the off-duty hours (Fig. 21).

Larger forts might have a hospital, with wards arranged to either
side of a central corridor, and workshops for the repair of vehicles,
weapons and tools.

Roman forts on the Scottish frontier often had attached to them
annexes, that is enclosures defended by a rampart and ditch, on one
or more sides of the fort. Such annexes have not been excavated
extensively, but where examined they have been found to contain
hearths and ovens, and workshops for industrial activities, as well as

21. **Leisure and recreation.** Gaming board from Bearsden; counters from Newstead; part of a *strigil* (for scraping off dirt and sweat) from Bar Hill; unguent pots from Balmuildy.(Photo: Hunterian Museum).

religious shrines and sometimes, as already indicated, the fort bath-house. We should not suppose that they were mere empty space.

The defences of a fort consisted of a rampart, usually of turf with (in the Antonine period) a stone foundation-course. Beyond (i.e. outside) the rampart were one or more ditches, usually about 3 m across and 1.5 m deep. Gaps were left in the ditch-circuit for roads leading into the fort. The fort-gates were substantial timber structures, usually with a tower above the gate-passage itself, or towers at either side (Fig. 17); in a few cases the gates were stone-built.

Outside the fort and its annexe some civilian structures could be expected, to house the families and slaves of the soldiers, friendly natives (some of whom could well have chosen to live for their own safety in the lee of the fort), and traders and storekeepers providing extra food, luxuries and various services to the soldiers of the garrison. Wine and women were presumably available at a price, and songs inspired by the former and describing the latter were doubtless to be heard. These little villages (*vici*) grew up along the roads leading away from the forts. We do not as yet know very much about such settlements in Scotland, although they are familiar to the visitor to Hadrian's Wall, for example at Vindolanda.

Fortlets

A very much smaller installation was the fortlet, designed to house 50 to 80 men at most in one or two barrack blocks. Fortlets usually had a single gate through the rampart, with a timber tower above, and one or two ditches beyond (Fig. 22). Fortlets are found in Scotland at intermediate points along major roads, or at river crossings. The fortlet at Oxton (below, p. 120; Fig. 69) had several annexes, including an enormous enclosure to the south. One particular type of fortlet appears on the Antonine Wall – seemingly at every mile there was a fortlet-type structure attached to the Wall itself; we call these small installations 'mile-fortlets' (below, p. 131). They match the mile-castles on Hadrian's Wall and served as intermediate control points along the frontier line.

Watch-towers

Mention should also be made of watch-towers: these were usually of timber, set within a low rampart and a single or double ditch, and spaced out along roads to observe traffic and population movement (Fig. 23). Most towers were some 3 m–4 m square at the base, and at least two storeys high. A causeway led through the ditch or ditches to the nearby road. These towers may have been manned by half a dozen men. We could easily worry about their safety in the event of a sudden attack by substantial hostile forces. Information would be passed by means of fire-signals or torches along a line of such posts to warn of danger. On the Gask Ridge in Perth & Kinross a regular sequence of towers seems to have served for a time to mark the outer limit of the Roman province in the Flavian period (below, p. 166).

Legionary fortresses

For the most part, after an initial conquest period, the legions returned to their bases in the south, while the auxiliaries in their

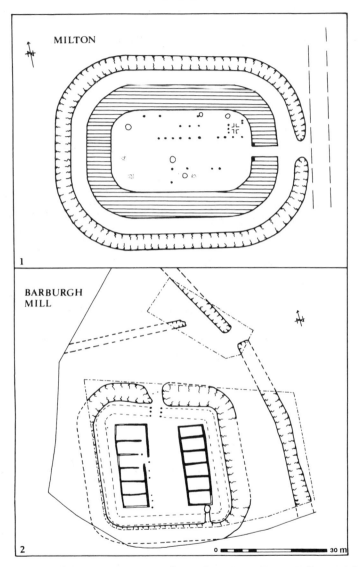

22. **Fortlets of the Antonine period**. 1. Milton, Dumfries & Galloway (after Clarke), showing postholes of internal buildings, within a rampart and single ditch; see also p. 88. 2. Barburgh Mill, Dumfries & Galloway (after Breeze), showing plans of two barracks within a rampart (outline restored) and a single ditch. The extra ditches to the N and E restricted access to the promontory on which the fortlet sat; see also p. 91.

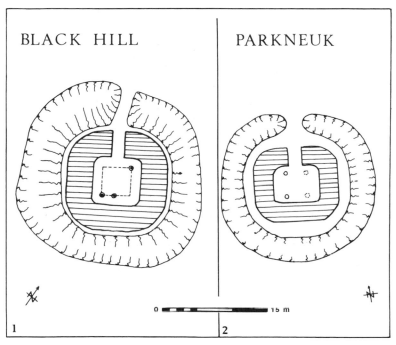

23. Watch-towers of the Flavian period. 1. Black Hill, Meikleour, Perth & Kinross (after Richmond): a tower 3.5 m (12 ft) square lay within a broad turf rampart and a single ditch; see also p. 181. 2. Parkneuk, Gask Ridge, Perth & Kinross (after Robertson). The tower 3 m (10 ft) square lay within a rampart and single ditch; see also p. 168.

forts remained scattered through the countryside and along lines of communication. Nevertheless, Scotland can boast of two legionary fortresses – at Inchtuthil on the Tay near Dunkeld (below, p. 178), and the much smaller site at Carpow on the southern side of the Tay estuary near Newburgh (below, p. 170). Inchtuthil belongs to the period of the Flavian occupation in the later first century and Carpow to the Severan advance in the early third. So far as we can tell, no legion was based in Scotland in the Antonine period, though some legionaries remained as garrisons in a few of the Antonine Wall forts, at Newstead and perhaps elsewhere.

A legionary fortress was a fort on a very large scale indeed; or rather the fort was a microcosm of the legionary base. The legionary

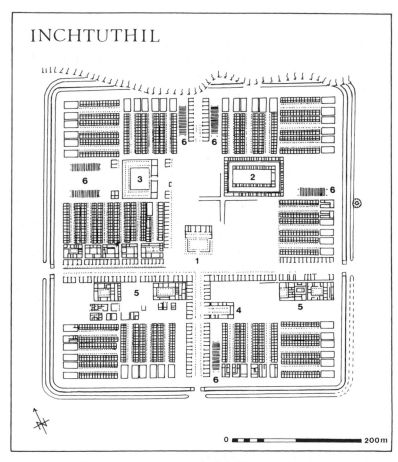

24. **Inchtuthil, Perth & Kinross:** ground-plan of a legionary fortress of the Flavian period (after Pitts and St Joseph). Note: 1 = headquarters, 2 = hospital, 3 = workshop, 4 = drill-hall(?), 5 = tribunes' houses, 6 = granaries. The remaining buildings are barracks. See also Fig. 99.

fortresses of the Roman world were about 20–25 ha. (50–60 acres) in size, and housed some 5000 men. The reader will recognise the main features of the layout of Inchtuthil (Fig. 24): headquarters building, granaries, store buildings, a hospital, and barracks in profusion, arranged in groups of six, reflecting the six centuries of the legionary cohort. Lacking at Inchtuthil is the commanding officer's house, evidently not yet built when the base was abandoned.

Roads

Of vital importance to the Roman control of a frontier area was a network of roads. 'All roads lead to Rome' is a familiar saying. More correctly all roads led from Rome, reaching out from the city to Italian towns and then to provincial centres and from there to the very frontiers of the Empire. In Britain the road system developed quickly in the aftermath of the Claudian conquest. Roads radiated from London, to the West Country, into the Midlands (Watling Street) and due northwards to York (Ermine Street). In Scotland the network of roads was determined by topographical necessities (below, p. 42), along the valleys still used for the most part by the modern road and rail networks. Roman roads are found today by recognition of their cambered mounds in the countryside, by observation on maps of the alignment of secondary roads, farm-tracks, or field boundaries, by the identification of placenames indicating old roads, and from the air – a whitish parched stripe indicating the presence of a gravel surface not far below the present-day ground-level, or quarry pits and drainage gullies extending into the distance across the landscape.

25. **Roman road** at Stonehouse, South Lanark, looking E along its embankment; the alignment is continued by the line of trees into the distance (Photo: L. Keppie). See also p. 107.

26. **Milestone**, from Ingliston, West Lothian, with the text restored (Photo: National Museums of Scotland). See also p. 41.

Excavation of a Roman road in Scotland reveals a fairly standard make-up: a lower stratum of large cobbles, some 6 m across, topped by small stones and gravel, and often flanked by side-ditches. Sometimes the road was set on a bed of turf, or placed directly on rock. The essentials of the road system must have been laid down by Agricola or his immediate successor: some lengths of road north of Perth must be dated to this time, as the area was seemingly not reoccupied in the Antonine period. Roman roads are proverbial for their straightness. But more often the road builders (usually soldiers) marked out a line in advance from one high point to another, after which there might be a change in alignment. By geographical necessity Roman roads in Scotland were often not straight, especially when following a river. Distances along the roads were marked by milestones, of which only one has survived from Scotland – at Ingliston near Edinburgh (Fig. 26). As Scotland had at least 500 miles of Roman road, many more milestones must await discovery.

Undoubtedly the coasts of Scotland would have witnessed Roman vessels engaged in trade or bringing supplies to the northern garrisons. Harbour facilities at Camelon, Cramond and elsewhere can be supposed, as well as smaller boats sailing along major rivers such as the Tweed; a wooden oar was among finds made at Newstead (below, p. 113).

5
THE MONUMENTS IN THE LANDSCAPE

For the Roman army, as much as for later English invaders and the modern tourist, the approaches to Scotland by land are strictly limited by, and must conform to, geographical factors. The modern traveller to Scotland, heading up the western side of the country, whether by road or rail, follows the valleys of the Annan and the Clyde to reach Glasgow (the A74/M74). On the eastern side of the country the traveller from Newcastle to the Forth at Edinburgh may follow the coast (the A1), or strike inland by way of Redesdale across Carter Bar to the Tweed Valley and then via Lauderdale to the Forth (the modern A68).

Further north the major arterial route (the A9/M9) runs from Falkirk to Stirling, then through Strathallan and Strathearn to the Tay at Perth. Thereafter the traveller must traverse the broad valley of Strathmore, noting always the heights of the Highland massif on his left, mountains which draw ever closer until the mouths of the Dee and the Don, after which the plains of Moray and Nairn come into view.

To the modern reader and traveller, with satellite pictures of Scotland available in every atlas, and Ordnance Survey maps providing an easy digest of available knowledge, such a statement on routes may seem obvious enough. The best way from Newcastle to Edinburgh, or Carlisle to the Clyde, may be obvious from an aircraft or even from an armchair, but the Romans had no such advantages. Dependent on reconnaissance parties, hearsay and features visible on the horizon, they proceeded to lay down the essentials of a communication system that has lasted until the present day.

The Romans did not think merely in terms of north–south communication in Scotland. A significant geographical, and indeed geological, factor in the make-up of the Scottish terrain is the sequences of hills that run north-east to south-west: the Cheviots, the Lammermuirs, the Pentlands south of the Forth, and further north the Ochils and the Highland massif. That the Romans in the Flavian period established a north-east to south-west defence line along the edge of the Highlands has long been evident. But south of the Forth their road network, both confirmed by actual survivals and restored by reasonable conjecture, suggests a number of lines running north-east to south-west, which may mark stages in advance or withdrawal, or at the very least of communication and control between tribal groupings, in the first and second centuries.

Many Roman installations are immediately recognisable on the ground or from the air. Forts, with their multiple ditches, 'playing-card' shape, rounded corners and regular street plans; camps with long straight single ditches, symmetrically placed gateways sometimes defended by *clavicula* or by traverse (above, p. 27); the roads with their confident alignment, quarry pits and side-ditches. But not every square enclosure need be a Roman fort or fortlet, and not every circular ditch seen from the air need enclose a Roman watch-tower. Rigorous modern research into the characteristics of field monuments has removed doubt in many cases, but it would be premature to claim that every archaeological site seen in the countryside or observed from the air can be instantly categorised. Proximity to a Roman road could decide in favour of a Roman date – yet a ditched enclosure at West Plean beside a Roman road north of Larbert, Falkirk, excavated in 1953–55 with a view to providing a plan of a Roman watch-tower, proved instead to be an Iron Age homestead. A ditched enclosure on Beattock Summit, South Lanarkshire, initially considered by some as a burial cairn, was found on excavation in 1966 to be a Roman watch-tower (below, p. 88). From the air such small enclosures, with a circular ditch interrupted by a single gap, may be hard to categorise. Square enclosures with sharp rather than round corners may prove to enclose Iron Age or medieval settlements or homesteads. Sometimes aerial reconnaisance can reveal sites of many different periods in close proximity: the same factors (well-drained ground, water supply, a river crossing) could bring not only Romans but prehistoric settlers, and motte- and castle-builders later. The Romans were not alone in building roads in Scotland: medieval hollow-ways and eighteenth-century metalled roads may run parallel to, or overlie or disrupt, the Roman system. Not every straight road need be Roman. Indeed one stretch of paved road with a central drain, descending a steep slope near Rochdale in Lancashire, which continues to feature as an illustration in books about Roman Britain, seems to have been laid down in 1734!

6

PIECING TOGETHER THE ROMAN PAST

The source material available for a study of the Romans in Scotland does not consist merely of literary works surviving from antiquity. We have already learned something of the archaeological evidence deriving from the excavated remains of forts and other installations. The process of excavation produces in addition a sometimes considerable quantity of artefacts in metal, stone, clay, glass and other materials, all of which can provide information to the historian or archaeologist and sometimes a fairly exact date when they were made. Some of these categories of finds deserve a detailed description.

Inscriptions

Particularly helpful towards our appreciation of the Roman period in Scotland are inscriptions. That is, stones on which have been inscribed some words or phrases in Latin. The language is not the literary Latin of Tacitus, Cicero or Vergil; the texts abound with semi-technical phrases of the military establishment. Words are often abbreviated, even to a single letter. Such abbreviations must, we may safely assume, have been comprehensible to Roman soldiers but may require some hard thinking for us to decipher today. Yet we too live in a world of abbreviations – some are perennial, for example a.m. and p.m. (derived from Latin); others are potentially shortlived, for example VAT or MOT, which in a generation or two will perhaps be all but forgotten, to remain only of mild antiquarian interest. Abbreviations were used on Latin inscriptions primarily to save space, so enabling the writer to maximise the content of the message on the limited flat area of stone available.

The most common categories of inscriptions surviving in Scotland are chiselled on *a.* commemorative stones recording building work; *b.* altars erected to gods and goddesses; and *c.* gravestones, chiefly of members of the Roman garrisons or their families (Fig. 27). Almost all the inscriptions known in Roman Scotland can be dated to the Antonine period, i.e. in the mid-second century AD.

Commemorative stones, the first category, are usually rectangular

27. **Inscribed stones from the Antonine Wall** (after Collingwood and Wright). 1. Distance slab from Kirkintilloch erected by men of the Sixth Legion; the actual length of the Wall completed by the legion was never inserted on the stone (Scale 1/24). 2. Altar from Auchendavy near Kirkintilloch, erected to the Presiding Spirit (*Genius*) of the Land of Britain by Marcus Cocceius Firmus, a centurion of the Second Legion (see also p. 148). Scale 1/16. 3. Gravestone from Shirva near Kirkintilloch, commemorating Flavius Lucianus, a soldier in the Second Legion. Scale 1/16. The original stones are in the Hunterian Museum.

in shape and relatively thin, and were intended to be inserted into the building whose construction they recorded. The inscription was placed on the front face of the stone, often within a moulded frame. One particular category of commemorative stones deserves a special mention: the so-called 'distance slabs' from the Antonine Wall, which record the lengths of wall-building work completed by the legionary detachments engaged on the task. Here the inscriptions begin with a dedication to the Emperor Antoninus Pius, then give the numeral and

28. **Distance slab,** from Hutcheson Hill on the Antonine Wall, erected by men of the Twentieth Legion to record the completion of 3000 feet of the work (Photo: Hunterian Museum).

the titles of the legion responsible, and end with the precise distance completed, in paces or in feet (see Figs. 27.1, 28–29).

A second category of stones is *altars*, squat squared-off pillars which bear an inscription to the god or goddess being venerated (Fig. 27.2). The top of an altar was hollowed out to form a *focus* or miniature hearth where fruit might be piled as an offering. The dedicator then poured wine or milk on top. On large altars a fire might be lit in the focus to consume the offerings, but it is evident that the *focus* on many altars is too small to have served that purpose – the hollow was merely symbolic. Sometimes, if the occasion was sufficiently important or the dedicator sufficiently wealthy, an animal might be sacrificed, and its entrails examined.

Altars (Figs. 27.2, 30) were not normally erected on the spur of the moment. What happened was that someone (an individual or a group) might promise an altar to a god, if the god gave some help in a time of need – for example to Neptune before a sea-crossing or to Mars before a battle. If the desired help was forthcoming and

29. **Distance slab** from Hutcheson Hill on the Antonine Wall: central scene showing Britannia (?) in the act of presenting a laurel wreath to the Eagle of the Twentieth Legion held by its standard-bearer (Photo: Hunterian Museum).

the person came safely through the expected ordeal, he erected an altar in fulfilment of the promise. The inscription first named the god to whom the dedication was being made, then the names of the dedicators (if a whole military unit set up the altar, the commanding officer's name was often given), and ended with the standard formula *votum solvit laetus libens merito* (almost always abbreviated to the letters V.S.L.L.M.): 'gladly, willingly and deservedly fulfilled his vow'; i.e. the vow to erect the altar which had been made when the god's help was first asked for.

The deities commemorated in this way might be the gods and goddesses of the Roman world – such as Jupiter, king of the gods,

30. **Sacrifice at an altar.** A scene from the distance slab found at Bridgeness (See also Fig. 7). Here officers and soldiers of the Second Legion (note flag in background with name and numeral of the legion) offer sacrifice, probably to Mars, to ask for the god's support in the forthcoming campaign (Photo: National Museums of Scotland).

Juno his wife, Mars, god of war, or Minerva, goddess of valour (Fig. 31). Sometimes more exotic gods of the eastern Mediterranean and beyond are found venerated on the northern frontier in Britain. These eastern deities offered a more exciting concept of religion, and rituals in which the individual had a definite role. At other times the dedications are to the local Celtic deities of the woodland and the stream. Auxiliary regiments dedicated altars to the deities of their homelands far away; for example, at Birrens in Dumfriesshire, the Second Cohort of Tungrians, originally from Belgium, set up altars

31. **Altar to Disciplina,** erected by the Second Cohort of Tungrians; from Birrens, Dumfries & Galloway (Photo: National Museums of Scotland). See also p. 82.

to the outlandish-sounding goddesses Viradecthis and Ricagambeda. Sometimes Roman and Celtic deities were worshipped together: at Bar Hill on the Antonine Wall a cohort of Syrian archers from the town of Hama on the River Orontes put up a dedication to Mars Camulus, the Roman and Celtic war-gods combined as a single personage. From Croy Hill on the Antonine Wall there is a dedication to Jupiter Dolichenus, that is to the Syrian god of the heavens equated with Jupiter; such was the all-embracing and cosmopolitan nature of religious belief in antiquity (cf. Fig. 32).

Gravestones form a third category of inscription. The text is usually quite short: the name of the deceased and his military unit, perhaps the number of years served and the age at death (Fig. 27.3). Sometimes

32. **Statuette of Brigantia,** tutelary goddess of the Brigantes tribe of northern England; from Birrens, Dumfries & Galloway (Photo: National Museums of Scotland). Brigantia has been given the attributes of several classical goddesses. She wears a turreted crown, symbolising her protective role, the weapons and gorgon-medallion of the goddess Minerva, the wings of Victory and the globe and navel-stone (bottom left) of Celestial Juno. This statuette is an excellent example of the amalgamation of attributes so common in Roman religion.

the inscription may be accompanied by a full-length sculptured representation of the deceased, in uniform. The gravestones were frequently erected along the roads leading away from forts.

The gravestones marked the last resting place of the body – or more usually the ashes – of the deceased, cremation being the normal rite at this time. Gravestones cost money, and not everyone could afford them; the ashes might simply be placed in a glass jar or in an

33. **Cremation burial in a pot,** found at Croy Hill on the Antonine Wall, 1976 (Photo: Hunterian Museum).

earthenware pot (Fig. 33), with a wooden marker, or none at all, at ground level. Soldiers contributed, it seems, during their military service to a burial-club which ensured proper commemoration if the need arose.

It should be emphasised that not every inscription survives complete – sometimes only a fragment is found with a few letters legible, where the message breaks off tantalisingly in mid-word or -phrase. Some stones reported by antiquaries can no longer be found, or the inscription cannot now be read after prolonged exposure to rain and frost. Several stones found long ago were built into farmhouses, and perished when the latter were rebuilt in Victorian times or later.

Not every Latin inscription was chiselled on stone: words could be scratched on pots, stamped on tiles, or engraved on glass and metal. Samian pottery (below, p. 54) often bears the name of the maker or his factory, as do *mortaria* (mixing bowls); amphorae often have a stamp on the rim or handle indicating the name of the estate or its owner, where the contents – oil or wine – were produced. Sometimes the owners of pots wrote their own names on the side, or scratched a mark to indicate the current contents – for example VIN for *vinum* (wine). From Carpow comes an amphora with a graffito which seems to indicate that the contents were flavoured with horehound, evidently as a cough mixture, no doubt much in demand on the cold northern frontier. Such casual scribblings often cast a highly informative light.

Coins

Many families in Britain today have a Roman coin somewhere at home, perhaps several, to show to children and visitors as relics of a past era; sometimes these are coins found in Scotland itself, but others have been brought back from abroad, some by returning servicemen, or bought in antique shops or markets. Coins were first brought to Scotland in bulk by the Roman soldiers of the invasion army, and by commissariat staff who used them to pay for materials and foodstuffs purchased locally (Fig. 34). Roman coins bore on the obverse (heads) side the profile of the reigning emperor, and on the reverse (tails) side perhaps the outline of a newly completed public building, for example the Colosseum in Rome, which was opened to the public in AD 80 while Agricola was in Scotland – a Caledonian bear, perhaps furnished through the agency of Agricola's army, was among the attractions at the inaugural games – or the news of some military victory or information about the imperial family. Coins served like our postage stamps today as a digest of important events. They were a convenient method of propagating news to the population of a far-flung empire. Round the edge of the coin was a Latin inscription giving on the obverse the names and titles of the emperor, and the magistracies he had held or was then holding, and on the reverse some brief message, just an abbreviated word or two, explaining the scene portrayed.

Sometimes the events reported on the reverses of coins referred to events in Britain or victories won there. Thus the successes of Lollius Urbicus' army in Scotland in AD 142–43 prompted the issue

34. **Bronze arm-purse, with a selection of coins.** The purse was found at Croy Hill in 1978 (Photo: Hunterian Museum).

of coins showing *Britannia* reclining on rocks, and others of a winged Victory-figure and the letters BRITAN. Similarly the achievements of the Emperor Septimius Severus and his son Caracalla in Britain in AD 208–11 were reported on their coins, with scenes showing Victory-figures piling up captured arms and the legend VICTORIAE BRITANNICAE, 'victories won over the Britons'.

Coins are found on excavations of Roman sites in Scotland, but not in large numbers. Others are casual finds, from gardens or ploughed fields. Nowadays many coins found each year are located by metal detectorists. Most of the coins found in the ground are very corroded and need expert attention if they are to be identified and dated and not to disintegrate from handling and from contact with the air. Numerous coin hoards have come to light; some could represent the savings of individual soldiers, but others may be loot taken by natives or represent subsidies paid out to tribal leaders by the Romans to secure peace on the northern frontier (cf. below, p. 188). Their burial may signal periods of uncertainty and crisis on the frontier, as does the failure to retrieve them.

Pottery

Inscriptions and coins were not the only Roman artefacts left behind in Scotland. A visitor walking over a Roman site is most likely to pick up fragments of pottery brought to the surface by ploughing. On an excavation the pottery will form the bulk of the finds made during the dig. What we see is the crockery of the barrack room and the cooking area. Of all Roman pottery the most distinctive is so-called samian ware, which was imported to Britain from central and southern France. The name 'samian' results from a mistaken inference made long ago about its place of manufacture, then believed to be the Greek island of Samos. Samian ware was made in many standard shapes: cups, plates and bowls (the latter often decorated

35. **Table ware.** Bronze jug from Lesmahagow, and samian vessels (Photo: Hunterian Museum).

36. **Cooking vessels.** *Mortarium* (mixing bowl), jars and dishes (Photo: Hunterian Museum).

with embossed designs). It is frequently possible to assign even the smallest fragment to a particular type of vessel, so standardised were the shapes (Fig. 35).

Another common find is the *mortarium*, a heavy-rimmed bowl used for mixing and crushing vegetables. In shape and function it resembles the modern ceramic baking-bowl, but was clearly not used for baking: the interior had a coating of rough quartz-grit which helped to break down vegetables, but wore away in time and must have ended up in the food itself.

Equally distinctive is the bulbous amphora, with its strong handles and broad rim, the bulk container of antiquity (it held about 27 litres/ 6 gallons). The amphorae found in Britain came mostly from southern Spain, and were used to export that country's most plentiful products, olive oil (for cooking) and wine.

In addition Roman soldiers and civilians had available a wide range of jars and cooking pots, among them 'black-burnished ware' made in Dorset and in Essex. Pottery kilns have been found at several forts in Scotland, indicating that supplies from the south might be supplemented with wares produced locally as the demand arose (Fig. 36).

Miscellaneous small finds

An excavation is likely also to yield some ironwork – brackets, hinges and the like, and very frequently nails. There may also be objects of bronze: belt-fittings, horse-trappings and brooches. Lead was used, as in modern times, for piping. Frequently too there is glass – mainly from window panes, in a shiny blue-green colour, clear on one side and frosted on the other; less frequently small fragments of glass bottles and cups are found; needless to say these must have been easily broken. Finally the archaeologist on an excavation or the walker over a ploughed field may find fragments of roofing tiles in a hard red clay, and bricks and tiles, often the wreckage of a heating system (above, p. 33). Luxury items too may be found – finger rings with engraved gemstones set into them, or jewellery in glass, silver or gold. A few wooden objects may also be recovered during excavation, preserved in wet conditions, the remnants of a wide range of structural timbers, fitments, furniture and personal belongings which have crumbled away over the centuries. Complete wagon-wheels have been found at Bar Hill and at Newstead. Leather too can survive if the surroundings are sufficiently damp: both Newstead and Bar Hill have produced shoes by the score, and we may also see today in museums leather panels from soldiers' tents, and fragments of clothing and shield covers.

When isolated finds are made, the finder often (though unfortunately not always) brings the material to a museum or to an archaeologist who will be able to identify it. All genuine finds – and of course not every object believed by its finder to be Roman is that old or was actually unearthed in Scotland – are reported in *Discovery and Excavation in Scotland*, a yearly magazine published by the Council for Scottish Archaeology, through which the information is disseminated to a wider public. Finds may be made by walkers in the countryside, or by farmers in newly ploughed fields, or by metal detector users. By law, finders are required to report discoveries to the police or to a museum; as a result finds may be claimed by the Crown under the Treasure Trove procedure, and a reward paid to the finder. Sometimes the finds are from known Roman sites – where a tree has blown over or a stream is eroding a bank or hillside; or are found completely in isolation where no known site exists. Individual discoveries may seem isolated, but the archaeologist will know whether there is a Roman site nearby. Sometimes apparently isolated finds are shown years later to derive from a Roman fort which was not yet located when the find was made: the find itself may be the first indicator of the existence of a site. Yet every find should not be taken to indicate a Roman installation: sometimes coins or potsherds, finger rings or brooches were lost beside a road, the result of traffic along it. Or the material may prove to derive from a village or homestead of the contemporary local population, who had obtained Roman goods, as gifts or bribes, by exchange or barter, as they became aware of the proximity of the manufactured goods of the Roman common market (below, p. 70). Roman material reached the houses and settlements of the indigenous tribes not only within the areas under the army's control; Roman objects are found in the far north, in the Outer Isles and in Orkney and Shetland, the result of trade and contact over many hundreds of miles.

7

THE REDISCOVERY OF
ROMAN SCOTLAND

Today we are familiar with the modern names of many archaeological sites and their precise dating within the Roman period. But for the antiquaries of several centuries ago, the picture was much less clear.

Already by the fall of the Roman Empire in the fifth century AD, historians were becoming confused about who had actually built walls in Britain and where they were. But gradually, with the rediscovery at the Renaissance of classical manuscripts in the monasteries of continental Europe, it could be seen that Scotland had indeed been invaded and occupied on a number of occasions. Early Scottish historians endeavoured to reconcile popular tradition with the newly available literary evidence. Even the location of the Antonine Wall remained a matter of dispute until the 1690s, when an inscribed stone bearing the name of Lollius Urbicus was seen at Balmuildy fort. This stone, claimed antiquarian Alexander Gordon in 1726, was 'the most invaluable Jewel of Antiquity that ever was found in the Island of

37. 'The most invaluable Jewel of Antiquity' (Alexander Gordon, 1726). Commemorative slab from Balmuildy fort on the Antonine Wall, recording construction work by the Second Legion during the governorship of Quintus Lollius Urbicus. The text is restored (Photo: Hunterian Museum).

Britain' (Fig. 37). Today's students would be amazed to think that the siting of the Wall, between Clyde and Forth, had ever been in doubt. Standing monuments were often assigned to the wrong archaeological periods, as were small finds. A number of old bridges in southern Scotland, for example those at Bothwellhaugh and Duntocher, were designated 'Roman' by local tradition, in error.

By the early seventeenth century Latin inscriptions were being read and their texts published; the standing remains were being identified on the ground. The eighteenth century was a period of great antiquarian activity. In 1726 Alexander Gordon published his *Itinerarium Septentrionale* ('Journey through the North') which recorded in set sequence many Roman sites in Scotland, with sketch-plans of the sites and drawings of associated antiquities. This volume was followed shortly by the ambitious and authoritative *Britannia Romana* of John Horsley whose survey covered all of Roman Britain, with particular emphasis on Hadrian's Wall and the North. The role of Scotland in the history of the Roman Empire was now firmly established.

Among Scottish antiquaries of this time the dominant figure was Sir John Clerk of Penicuik whose indefatigable efforts are recorded in correspondence with fellow enthusiasts; the outbuildings at Penicuik House soon overflowed with altars and inscribed stones purchased by his agents or sent to him by admirers and friends. Most passed in 1857 to the then National Museum of Antiquities in Edinburgh, and are now in the Museum of Scotland.

The aftermath of the second Jacobite Rebellion of 1745 brought to Scotland a young surveyor of the first order, William Roy, who assisted in the laying out of new roads to control the Highlands; he also worked on the preparation of a large-scale map of Scotland. Roy noted the surviving earthworks of many sites he recognised as of Roman origin, and had them accurately planned; the end product was *The Military Antiquities of the Romans in Britain*, published posthumously in 1793. Many of the sites drawn under Roy's direction are now badly eroded or even afforested, so that his survey may supply details long since lost. The zest for antiquarian discovery is reflected in Sir Walter Scott's novel, *The Antiquary*, published in 1816. At one point the hero, Jonathan Oldbuck, proudly displays to a visitor the battlefield of *Mons Graupius* which lay, he claimed, on his own estate.

The antiquaries of the eighteenth and nineteenth centuries put together their picture of Roman Scotland mainly by the observation and recording of standing monuments, together with an account of the finds, especially inscribed stones and coins, made at each site over the years. But, surprisingly perhaps to the modern reader, they did not, with a very few exceptions, dig in search of information. The pen, the measuring chain and the surveyor's pole were their tools, not the spade, the trowel or the brush. Perhaps we should be grateful for this – most sites were left alone until more recent methods became available. The 1890s brought a decisive change. A committee of the Glasgow Archaeological Society carried out a modest programme of work along the line of the Antonine Wall in 1890–93, to confirm its alignment and examine its constituent parts. The resulting *Antonine Wall Report* (Glasgow, 1899) remains a valuable account. In 1895 the Society of Antiquaries of Scotland established a committee to plan and carry out excavations on selected important sites, and within a ten-year period large-scale work took place at many forts, including Inchtuthil, Lyne, Castlecary and Camelon (Fig. 38). The results received prompt publication in the *Proceedings of the Society of Antiquaries of Scotland*. Much was learned in a short span of time.

In the twentieth century excavation continued apace. Special mention can be made of the work of Sir George Macdonald at several Antonine Wall sites and elsewhere, which culminated in his *Roman Wall in Scotland* (second edition, Oxford, 1934). Sir Ian Richmond dug with masterly brilliance at Fendoch and Inchtuthil, and at many other sites north and south of the Antonine Wall. The late Professor Anne Robertson worked at Castledykes, Duntocher, Birrens and Cardean. Their successors have maintained the momentum.

Emphasis has shifted from excavation purely for the purposes of gaining information, to 'rescue' archaeology, on sites threatened by destruction from modern development, whether for oil pipelines, roads, factories or housing projects. In contrast to the situation of little more than a decade ago, when the taxpayer footed the bill, the majority of digs are now financed by those who will stand to gain by the development. Archaeological 'companies' or 'units' have been formed to tender for such work. Excavation has become an extremely expensive activity, with the employment of mechanical excavators to speed the process when time (or rather the lack of it) is an important factor. The costs of post-excavation work are high too, now that the botanist, the soil scientist, the conservation technician and a variety of specialist workers can be recruited to study the small finds and

38. **Antiquaries examining a newly found Roman torso,** at Camelon, 1905 (Photo: Falkirk Museums).

ecological setting of the site. As the techniques of excavation have improved, the process of digging has paradoxically slowed. New sites are being found faster than they can possibly be excavated, so that there is no danger of present-day archaeologists running out of projects.

The number of known sites has expanded enormously, and new discoveries seem likely to continue at an undiminished rate. Gaps are being filled on the map of Roman Scotland, new roads are being identified, and the whole picture of occupation appears more intense. New sites are still found by observation on the ground, as in past decades, by the dedicated fieldworker, following a fine tradition exemplified by O.G.S. Crawford, one-time Archaeology Officer of

39. Glenlochar, Dumfries & Galloway. Outline of the Roman fort showing as a crop-mark, seen from the W (Photo: Ministry of Defence, British Crown Copyright Reserved).

the Ordnance Survey. Many more sites have, however, been identified from the air.

The realisation that ancient sites might be visible from the air when nothing could be seen at ground level developed in the inter-war years as the potential of the aerial survey was perceived. The Second World War saw an improvement in techniques, and postwar examination of many photographs taken for military purposes revealed a plethora of archaeological sites. An annual programme of flying was initiated by Professor J.K.S. St Joseph to cover much of Britain. In Scotland Professor St Joseph added by his own efforts well over 20 forts and fortlets and dozens of marching camps to the map (Fig. 39). Observation from the air was followed by the testing of the sites on the ground by carefully placed trenches. St Joseph's work has been continued by the Royal Commission on the Ancient and Historical Monuments of Scotland.

Ancient sites can show up from the air because raking sunlight accentuates the faint remains of ramparts and ditches, which may be all that survive at ground level. Alternatively a light coating of snow may highlight the ancient features, or the differential melting of that snow may reveal a pattern. Much more common are what are called 'cropmark' sites, where certain features, especially ditches, show up from the air because of differential growth in a crop. The reason for this difference is that ditches dug long ago into the ground to defend a camp or fort attract water and moisture, so that at the height of summer when the crop – barley or wheat, even vegetables – is ripening, those parts of the crop overlying the now vanished ditches will grow thicker and higher, and remain unripened for a few days, perhaps a few weeks, longer than the rest of the field (Fig. 40). From the air, the line of the ditch shows up as a green strip in the field where

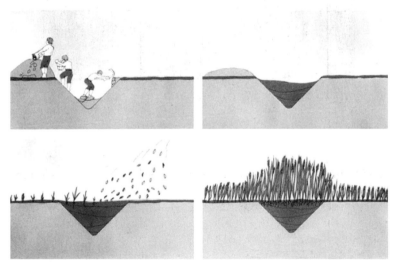

40. **The formation of crop-marks.** 1. A ditch is dug out and earth used to create a rampart. 2. The ditch fills up (or is filled in) over the centuries. 3. A farmer plants a crop. 4. Seeds planted over the line of the ditch grow better because of the extra moisture below (Hunterian Museum. After an original drawing by Maggie Wallace).

everything else has turned a golden yellow or begun to wither. It would be difficult to overstate the contribution of aerial photography to our knowledge of Roman Scotland. Yet it is perhaps not always easy for the general public to perceive its importance, when the end product of the investigation is not pottery, stone structures or the like, but a photographic print, in which certain lines and blobs are proclaimed significant by the finder and others dismissed as drainage ditches, hayricks and geological features. But photographs may speak eloquently of the impact of the Roman presence in Scotland, especially when a whole fort may be brought within our view, with its rounded corners, its gates, the orderly lines of streets and buildings (Fig. 39), all this when nothing may be seen at ground level and no excavation has ever been undertaken at the site. Given the ever-spiralling costs of excavation, aerial reconnaissance has proved an economical method of identifying new sites.

Increasing use is made also of geophysical survey which has yielded much new information on fort plans and adjacent settlements; a comprehensive programme of geophysical survey of Flavian forts north of the Tay is underway, under the direction of Dr D.J. Woolliscroft, as part of the Roman Gask Project. The correlating of data involving GIS (Geographic Information Systems) and three-dimensional mapping are being undertaken by RCAHMS. Archaeology is an ever-popular subject for television programmes: even as these pages were being revised, Channel 4's *Time Team* was investigating the fort at Drumlanrig (below, p. 93).

8
LIFE ON THE FRONTIER

What can we say about life on Rome's most northerly frontier? Throughout the periods of Roman rule, Scotland was under a military occupation, so that much of what we know relates to army personnel in their official duties and off-duty moments.

Life in forts in Roman Scotland, and on the Antonine Wall, was surely like that endured by defenders of frontiers anywhere – isolated and uneventful, or like army service today likely to consist of long periods of inaction punctuated by short spasms of intense activity, exhilaration and danger. This excess of inactivity was guarded against by Roman commanders who devised a number of expedients to counter it: route marches, arms training, practising the building of ramparts and the digging of ditches, even mock battles. It was this attitude of professionalism that made the Roman army superior to its opponents for so long. A degree of alertness had to be simulated

41. **Granary at Bearsden** on the Antonine Wall: artist's reconstruction of the interior (Hunterian Museum. Drawn by Sheila Lawson).

42. **Altar from Carriden**, recording a dedication to Jupiter, by the *vikani* (villagers) of the fort of *Velunia* (Photo: National Museums of Scotland).

when the army was converted to a frontier police force with every risk of staleness; but whether it was consistently achieved over long periods may be doubted.

We can build up from the archaeological assemblage a picture of life in the forts themselves: the crockery used, the food eaten and the living conditions (Fig. 41). Analysis of sewage deposits at Bearsden has provided information on the soldiers' diet (below p. 153). In general the soldiers lived on dairy and cereal products (the corn being ground down on the hand-querns each squad of men had at its disposal, to produce bread), with vegetables, nuts, oysters, mussels and whelks, fruit, fish and some meat; for the latter, evidence has survived in the form of animal bones recovered on excavations. The soldiers ate mutton and beef, bacon, even boar and deer, either boiled in bronze saucepans, or roasted on a spit. Wine was drunk, and beer.

Attitudes of mind are less easy to pinpoint. Seldom have we in Scotland the insights provided by papyri recovered from the dry sands of Egypt. Revelations about life at Vindolanda behind Hadrian's Wall, surviving on thin wooden writing-tablets preserved in damp, anaerobic conditions, are particularly informative: the food consumed, the requests written, hopes expressed and dashed. For Scotland we have as yet no specific written evidence of this sort – though the few graffiti show the potential for the recovery of some non-official corrective to the standard picture.

Outside many forts on Hadrian's Wall extensive villages grew up housing the soldiers' families, and offering various diversions from the stale round of military duties. But in Scotland such settlements, so far as we are aware, appear to have attained substantial size at only a few forts such as Inveresk, Cramond and Newstead. On the Antonine Wall itself excavation has yielded little evidence to add to epigraphic discoveries of long ago: a woman Verecunda and a civilian, Salamancs (or Salmanes), of likely eastern origin, perhaps a trader, attested on tombstones found at Shirva in 1726–31. The discovery in 1956 of an altar at Carriden fort (below, p. 132) testified to the presence of villagers (*vikani*) who jointly dedicated an altar to Jupiter under the supervision of a man called Aelius Mansuetus (Fig. 42). Clearly future discoveries will enhance our knowledge of frontier society, but it remains important not to overestimate the size of these extramural communities.

We can only guess at the general round of duties, though documents from other parts of the Roman Empire provide a helpful framework: the departure of patrols to the more remote valleys, anxiety for their safe return, standards seen gleaming in the distance presaging the return of the patrol to the delight of wives and children; carousals in the tavern – most of the troops were Celts, with a love of beer rather than wine; business deals struck with local natives; the onset of winter with the roads blocked by snow – and no ploughs on Beattock Summit or Carter Bar to keep them open; the news of an attack on an isolated fortlet beaten back or (much worse) successful; the death of an emperor, the swearing-in ceremony before the images of his successor, new messages and faces on the coins in the soldiers' pockets and purses; the essential sameness of frontier life for those who by choice or circumstances were destined to endure it; pay-days (every three months) accompanied by a parade; the arrival of a new centurion or prefect (higher officers enjoyed a mobility denied to 'other ranks'); new faces in the bath-house; the chance of special duty in another province, or beyond the frontier; limited leave (but how soldiers chose to spend it eludes us); hunting expeditions; death by disease or accident, after a quarrel, even by combat against the enemy; for the fortunate, survival to the date of discharge, often followed by voluntary settlement in close proximity to the frontier where ties were strongest and a homeland left behind half a lifetime before was all but forgotten.

9
THE IMPACT OF ROME

If we come to estimate the impact of the Romans on Scotland, we are bound to suppose that in the short term it was dramatic and devastating, at least for that part of the population which stood in the path of the invading army, or resisted its advance. The advent of the military forces of the Mediterranean world's superpower cannot but have created a tremendous impression.

How much resistance was actually offered is less easy to estimate. Tacitus asserts that Agricola was held up by bad weather in southern Scotland in AD 79, not by enemy opposition. Only north of the Forth-Clyde line did the army come under attack from the tribes of Caledonia. We know nothing meaningful from any literary source about the campaigns of Lollius Urbicus. The distance slabs can depict scenes of combat, but these may be symbolic. Certainly the army of Severus had to fight, but he had penetrated beyond the floodtide of the Antonine advance into Caledonia where hostility to Rome could be expected.

Archaeologically the impact of the Roman advance is also hard to pinpoint. If we suppose that the tribes resisted, we could look for signs of Roman retaliation or reduction of their strongholds. But even where some evidence of fires has been recovered during excavation, we cannot be certain that it resulted from Roman intervention rather than an accidental conflagration, or the inter-tribal warfare of which Tacitus writes. However, the excavator of the broch at Leckie near Stirling believes that the site was stormed by a Roman force in AD 142, after which the structure was demolished almost to ground level.

It would have been normal Roman practice to seek the cooperation of the tribal nobility at the time of the invasions, or before, with offers of citizenship and imperial favour, in return for prompt declarations of allegiance and continued loyalty. Whether these methods were tried in Scotland, and what measure of success they enjoyed, we cannot say. The tribal area of the Damnonii was seemingly bisected by the Antonine Wall, with one part remaining inside the frontier and the other part beyond. The Votadini, it is alleged by scholars, enjoyed a favourable status: their hillfort at Traprain Law in East

Lothian continued as a centre of population, or at least of power, with a surge of Roman luxury products attesting to its wealth and prosperity. Brooches and other products were manufactured at the site. A considerable quantity of silver tableware, in part flattened as bullion and with some pieces stamped with Christian symbols, was found on the hill in 1919. This 'Traprain Treasure' is likely to have reached northern Britain about AD 400, perhaps as an inducement to the local chieftain to remain loyal.

Evidence for native settlement underlying or immediately adjacent to Roman sites has been growing in recent years; we can now instance Bothwellhaugh, Camelon, Cappuck, Cargill, Carronbridge and Elginhaugh. Ploughmarks indicating agriculture in pre-Roman times have been found below several forts.

The sudden arrival of troops who needed to be clothed and fed would have a substantial effect on the local economy. At first the army brought up its own clothing, leatherwork, shoes and crockery from the south, but it would be natural to suppose that more and more local produce would be purchased at the fort-gates, or by individual soldiers who wished to supplement rations and obtain the products of local craftsmanship.

We can also suppose some effect on the local environment. Road building required stone and gravel, with a strip of land cleared to either side to provide visibility and protect travellers from sudden attack. The construction of forts made an even greater impact: timber was required in large quantities, and turf had to be cut. It has been estimated that a fort of 1.6 ha. (4 acres) would have required 22,000 cubic feet of timber to construct its internal buildings, towers and gates. The construction of the Antonine Wall is estimated to have used up a corridor of turf 50 m wide to both frontier and rear of the frontier line, assuming that suitable turf was available nearby. We have little secure information on the environment when the Romans arrived, but we should not suppose that it was entirely tree-covered, at least in the Lowlands. Botanical studies in the vicinity of the Antonine Wall suggest a landscape of heath and grassland, with the woodland cut back for the pasturing of animals. Whether the Roman presence did much to alter the traditional way of life for the great mass of the population may be doubted. We should not suppose that the tribesmen exchanged their cloaks for togas and began to speak Latin. Certainly this was the sequence in other provinces, but we cannot document it for Scotland. In essence, for Scotland the periods of occupation were too short, though the encouragement of chiefs to adopt a Roman lifestyle could be supposed. We know of few of the inhabitants of north Britain by names: Calgacus, the Caledonian war-leader at *Mons Graupius*, a nobleman Argentocoxus and his wife, exchanging views with Severus' wife, presumably in Britain, in the aftermath of the campaigns of AD 208–11, and Lossio Veda, grandson of Vapogenus, who made a dedication to the Emperor Alexander Severus (reigned AD 222–235) at Colchester in south-east England.

The Roman army had, however, no reason to suppose that its sojourn in Scotland, either in the later first century or mid-second century, would be brief. It was after all highly unusual for the Romans to withdraw from any territory overrun. But their withdrawal must certainly have shaken the confidence of native tribes and individuals who had sided too ostentatiously with the new masters. The decision to withdraw would have been followed by some demolition work. From Inchtuthil has come the famous hoard of almost one million mainly unused nails, buried below the floor of the fortress workshop, where they remained hidden from human gaze (and the hands of the local population) until 1956 (Fig. 43). Samian pottery and glass vessels from the stores were tipped into the drains, and smashed underfoot. Timber-framed barracks were dismantled and burnt. The sequence

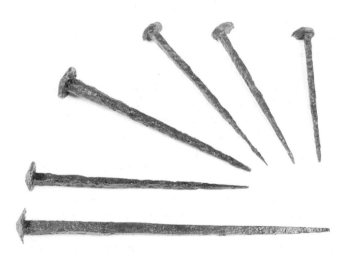

43. **Inchtuthil, Perth & Kinross:** iron nails found below the workshop. The longest nail measures 32 cms (Photo: Hunterian Museum).

is repeated at many forts where investigation allows a conclusion. At the close of the Antonine occupation, we know that at Bar Hill the headquarters building was carefully dismantled, with fitments and major structural timbers and stonework (column shafts and capitals) thrown into an adjacent well, a convenient repository.

The longer-term effects of Roman occupation seem to have been limited. The sites of forts, stripped of reusable materials, became overgrown and forgotten, except that place-name evidence can still provide clues: for example Kirkintilloch is originally the Gaelic Cairpentalloch, 'the fort at the end of the ridge'; Cramond is Caer Almond, 'the fort on the (River) Almond'. The road-system remained in use, until the cobbles wore away and the stones were dislodged; sometimes medieval hollow-ways followed the Roman route to one side. The English King Edward I marched northwards to Falkirk in 1298 by way of Dere Street, and in 1314 Robert Bruce before the battle at Bannockburn waited for the army of Edward II astride the Roman road northwards from Camelon towards Stirling. Roman stonework taken from forts was reused, in the fabric of castles such as Castle Cary close to the Antonine Wall and of ecclesiastical structures such as Jedburgh Abbey (below, p. 112)

It should not be imagined that the Roman presence in Scotland itself influenced the spread of Christianity – which came much later, with St Ninian, St Kentigern and St Columba in the fifth and sixth centuries.

The Latin language and the classical tradition have been two important factors in Scottish education, but the impulses were from the continent. Scots law is based directly (unlike English law) on the Roman system, but this has been a result of contacts with France and Italy during the Middle Ages and at the Renaissance, not from any memory of the Roman presence in Scotland itself.

There is a persistent (but fairly modern) Scottish tradition that Pontius Pilate, procurator (or, as we now know from an inscription, prefect) of Judaea at the time of the Crucifixion, was born at Fortingall in Perth & Kinross, while his father was in Scotland as a Roman emissary at the court of a local king. However, the story seems to lack any solid foundation. Fortingall itself lies beyond those Roman sites as yet identified in Perth & Kinross.

The conquest of Britain pulled the Romans further from their Mediterranean focus, to little clear advantage. If the modern Scot finds that London seems a long way from Edinburgh, and even further from the Highlands, let him consider the distance between Scotland and Rome, in an age of slow communications. Instead of bemoaning – or celebrating – the fate of Rome's Scottish endeavours, we should be surprised that they were ever contemplated at all. There is no doubt that the periods during which the Romans held southern and central Scotland were short. We can suppose a combination of factors which prompted the successive withdrawals: resistance and hostility to the imperialist aggressors, especially from tribes north of the Forth–Clyde line, to be set alongside the difficult terrain and harsh climate and in general the pointlessness of further expenditures of men and material to secure progressively poorer land, with little obvious economic return. Britain was always a fringe province of the Roman Empire.

PART TWO

VISITING SCOTLAND'S ROMAN REMAINS

Introduction

The following pages are designed to provide the visitor, whether by car or on foot, with a guide to the visible testimony to the Roman period in Scotland's past. The three main sections describe (1) Roman remains south of the Antonine Wall, from south to north; (2) the Antonine Wall itself, from east to west; and (3) Scotland north of the Antonine Wall, from south to north. If this sequence seems hard on those who, like the writer, live in the densest area of modern population in Scotland, the Glasgow conurbation, or those who live in the north-east, it can be pointed out that the Romans entered Scotland from the south, and it seems wisest to discover Scotland from the same direction as they did. In general each sub-section within the itineraries can be followed in a day or two of reasonable length by car. Obviously the cyclist or walker (who regrettably in these days is presumed to be in a minority) will take longer over the itineraries – by no means a bad thing. Finding a site and inspecting the surviving remains often take longer than expected, and advance preparation with suitable maps will save time on the day. Organisers of group visits are advised to check access for coaches in advance, which may on occasion present difficulties because of narrow roads or low bridges. Solid footwear and waterproof clothing against adverse weather conditions are always advisable, as some visits involve crossing mist-covered moorland and bog, forestry plantations or streams in full torrent. The carrying of a mobile phone (and a compass) is a wise precaution, as is leaving a visible note in one's car indicating route and destination. The author has vivid memories of being enveloped in mist, with only the noise from an invisible nearby motorway as an indicator of the return route, and of stepping without warning into deep forestry ditches. The visitor can expect to encounter cows, sheep, deer and, on occasion, a bull.

Visitors should recall that, while in Scotland there is no law of trespass as such, all land belongs to someone, and it is only sensible and courteous to enquire, even in this age of equality, at a nearby farmhouse or cottage to see if the owner is agreeable. This is especially so in more northerly parts, where gamekeepers may be unsympathetic to the unannounced visitor at certain times of the year. It is not the aim of this guide to alienate landowners and farmers who have in the past been amenable to archaeological exploration and endeavour. The inclusion of a site in this guide implies no guarantee of access or accessibility.

All but a few Roman sites in Scotland are scheduled under *The Ancient Monuments and Archaeological Areas Act* (1979); several forts and lengths of the Antonine Wall are 'guardianship monuments' in the care of the Scottish Executive and managed by Historic Scotland, as are a number of watchtowers on the Gask Ridge, Eagle Rock at Cramond, and some stretches of Dere Street.

An attempt has been made in the following pages to direct the visitor to those Roman sites in Scotland where something meaningful survives above ground. These sites are printed in bold type. Sites of some distinction in the Scottish context are marked by a single asterisk, and those of outstanding merit and impressiveness by two asterisks. The purpose of such grading is to direct the visitor, with a minimum of time, to see the best remains. All Roman sites in Scotland known to the author to the end of 2003 are marked on the accompanying maps (except for the construction camps along the Antonine Wall, and a temporary camp at Glenluce, too far to the west to be included on Fig. 44), though only those discussed in the following pages are individually named. For further information the reader is referred to the revised fourth edition of the *Ordnance Survey Map of Roman Britain* (1991). Details on access are generally given only for those sites where there is something definite to see. In general the accompanying Figures show only those Roman roads confirmed by the Ordnance Survey; other stretches tentatively identified over the years are noted annually in *Discovery and Excavation in Scotland*.

Ideally the visitor should aim to carry Ordnance Survey 1:50,000 maps of a particular area, and the check-list below (at pp. 200ff) provides a six-figure NGR (National Grid Reference) for all sites highlighted. An AA or RAC handbook will not suffice. The old OS quarter-inch maps, which show clearly mountains, river valleys and other important geographical features, provided a useful insight into why Roman roads and installations were placed in particular localities, so that the whole network of sites should begin to make more sense. For the Antonine Wall the Ordnance Survey historical map (HMSO 1969) is long since out of print. For the sake of consistency, the dimensions of camps and forts are given according to the figures available in the *Tabula Imperii Romani* (see Bibliography, p. 200), except where more recent work has clarified their extent.

The reader will find below no references to 'opening hours' of the sites described. Most lie in open farmland, and even those which are in government care can be visited at will, without charge.

It is not a particular purpose of this guide to describe even a selection of contemporary or near-contemporary Iron Age settlements, although some sites receive mention where they lie in close proximity to Roman installations, or have yielded a substantial number of Roman finds. The reader may be usefully referred to A. and G. Ritchie, *Scotland: an Archaeological Guide* (Oxford, 1998).

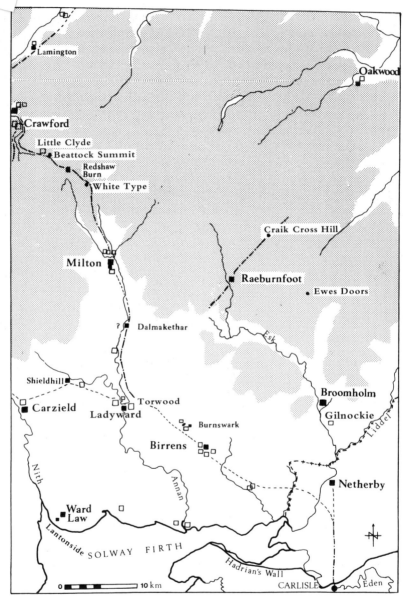

44. Annandale and Eskdale.

Lamington

Oakwood

Crawford

Little Clyde

Beattock Summit

Redshaw
Burn

White Type

Craik Cross Hill

Milton

Raeburnfoot

Ewes Doors

Dalmakethar

Esk

Shieldhill

Broomholm

Carzield

Torwood

Gilnockie

Ladyward

Burnswark

Liddel

Birrens

Netherby

Nith

Annan

Ward
Law

Lantonside SOLWAY FIRTH

Hadrian's Wall

CARLISLE

Eden

0   10 km

10

SCOTLAND SOUTH OF THE ANTONINE WALL

Annandale

For the Romans, as for later invaders and the modern traveller, the route to the north started at Carlisle, and led to the Dumfriesshire Esk at Netherby (where there was a fort in the grounds of Netherby House) and then into Annandale. The first major Roman site within the modern political boundaries of Scotland was at **Birrens***. (Turn off the A74(M) at the B7076 for Ecclefechan; double back across the carriageway at two roundabouts, then follow the B725 to Middlebie. Turn sharp right in Middlebie itself, on a road signposted to Eaglesfield, and just after the road passes between two cottages look for a stopping place on the right at a finger-post and stile. The fort platform is immediately in view; the visitor first arrives at its NE

45. **Birrens, Dumfries & Galloway:** aerial view of the Antonine fort from the SE (Photo: Ministry of Defence, British Crown Copyright Reserved).

46. **Burnswark, Dumfries & Galloway:** aerial view showing the siege-camp S of the hillfort (Photo: Cambridge University Committee for Aerial Photography).

corner. Multiple ditches on the N side, crossed by a causeway, survive here as faint hollows. The fort was first built in the Flavian period, and several times reconstructed and enlarged in the Hadrianic and Antonine periods, and held up to about AD 180. The visible ramparts, belonging to the Antonine fort (of 2.07 ha./5.1 acres), stand to a height of 1 m. There are gaps for gateways on the W, N and E sides. The S end of the fort has been eroded by the adjacent Mein Water, a tributary of the Annan, so that no part of the defences survives here; exposed stretches of stonework, from barracks or stables, are currently marked off by an electric fence. No trace can be seen on the ground of internal buildings, which were completely excavated in 1895, though the regular layout can be observed from the air (Fig. 45); further work was carried out in 1937–38 and 1962–69. A substantial annexe, also containing stone buildings, lay to the W. Numerous altars and sculptured reliefs (now in Dumfries or Edinburgh) have been found at Birrens over the centuries, and during the 1895 excavations (Figs. 31–32); many testify to the activities of the Second Cohort of Tungrians, the garrison from AD 158 till the abandonment of the fort. Much stonework from Birrens, including fragments of two inscribed stones, was recently found incorporated in an early monastic site at Hoddom, 5 km to the W, before the latter was lost to quarrying.

Some 4 km to the NW of Birrens rises the imposing eminence of **Burnswark Hill****, its summit occupied by an Iron Age fort, whose ramparts are clearly seen (Fig. 46); occupation began in the seventh century BC. On the lower slopes to both N and S are Roman camps, evidently designed to house a force besieging the native fort. (From Birrens return to Middlebie and take the B725 W towards Ecclefechan; shortly before the road crosses the railway line, turn sharp right onto an unsignposted minor road. Soon after, Burnswark Hill with a plantation below its E peak comes into view ahead; keep heading towards the hill, and park where the road divides. Take the rough, sometimes muddy, track through the trees, before the gate to Burnswark farm; bear right to reach the hillfort at one of the gateways, from which the Roman camps are best viewed (Fig. 47). The camp on the N side of the Hill (best seen from the E summit which is marked by a cairn of small stones) is the less well preserved, but much of its somewhat irregular outline is clear, in front of a forestry plantation. That on the S flank is the better preserved: the camp-rampart facing the hill is interrupted by three entrances, in front of which are three circular platforms 20 m across (known in local tradition as the Three Brethren), sometimes considered as emplacements for artillery, but more probably traverses protecting the camp gateways. (Descend via a sliding fieldgate to the camp's N rampart which stands to a height of over 1 m with a deep ditch in front.) The S camp incorporates within its NE corner a pre-existing enclosure, evidently a Roman fortlet, which faced S and whose interior was later occupied by native houses. From here the rampart and ditch of the camp can be followed S and then W, past at least one gateway, to the SW corner, from which the farm track is again reached. Rabbit burrowing and animal erosion are a severe problem, exposing for example the make-up of the fortlet's S rampart. Excavation on the hilltop in 1898 and in the later 1960s revealed stone catapult-balls and lead sling-bullets evidently propelled into the fort from the Roman camps below.

At first sight Burnswark is Scotland's Masada, but some have doubted whether it witnessed a great siege, heroic defence and final sacrifice. There are no continuous siege-lines round the hill, and excavation on the summit in 1966–68 suggested that the defences were long disused when Roman missiles were directed into the interior. It is possible therefore that the camps, both showing signs of careful construction and extended occupation, served as a training area for troops, perhaps from Hadrian's Wall or from Birrens, and provided an

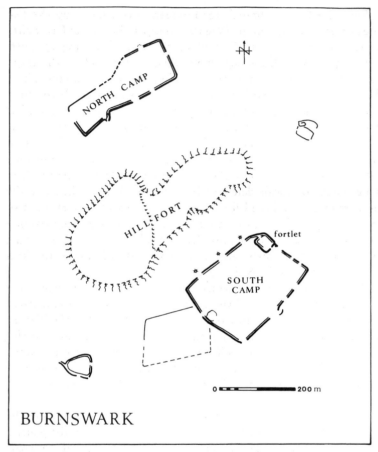

47. Burnswark, Dumfries & Galloway (after Jobey), showing the hillfort, with Roman siege-camps to N and S (the latter overlying a fortlet), and other earthworks nearby of uncertain date.

opportunity for peacetime artillery practice and the mock-storming of hillforts. Nevertheless the present author adheres to the traditional view of an actual, if brief, siege. Whatever explanation is preferred, the view from Burnswark Hill to the camps is an evocative reminder of the strength and discipline of the Roman army.

To the west of Gretna, away from any known Roman route, an apparently uninscribed Roman altar stands in farmland at Westhills, supported by piles of stones.

From Netherby a branch road evidently continued up the Esk. The ramparts of one camp along this route can be seen at **Gilnockie.** (From the A7 2 km N of Canonbie, turn right following signposts to Claygate. After the village is reached, continue along the B6318, signposted to Langholm. After 600 m look for a house on the left; at the next stretch of woodland take a track leftwards beside the trees. After 100 m a low bank with accompanying ditch is in view on the left side of the track. This is the E rampart of a 10-ha./25-acre camp.) The rampart can be followed across the field to the SE corner of the camp, then right into woodland; it survives as a low-spread bank 4 m wide and 0.5 m high. Just before the rampart enters the woodland, there is a gateway 20 m wide defended by a traverse. Within the wood the rampart can be followed for 350 m; there is a second gateway, also defended by a traverse; the rampart continues as a bracken-covered mound at the far end of the woodland, at which point the site of the SW corner of the camp is damaged by a now disused railway; the farm track itself overlies the N defences.

Further N along the Esk, at its junction with the Tarras Water, is a fort of 1.8 ha. (4.5 acres) at **Broomholm**, partly constructed on top of a native enclosure. The fort was initially constructed in the Flavian period. Later, perhaps under Hadrian, it was replaced by a fortlet, as an outpost for Hadrian's Wall. Occupation of the fortlet ended in destruction, followed by native reuse of the site. (Continue from Gilnockie along the B6318 till the road descends to cross the Tarras Water on a narrow bridge.

The fort lies on the plateau beyond. Some distance beyond the bridge, look for a fieldgate on the left. Walk uphill on to the plateau. An oblong fenced pond overlies the fort's NE corner. Continue across the plateau to the nearest visible telegraph pole.) Three ditches are visible here, defending the SW corner of the annexe of the Flavian fort, with a causeway across the ditches to reach a gate in the S side. A single ditch can be followed uphill along the fort's W side. On the hilltop, beyond a modern track defined by bankings, is a ditch on the N side of the fort, with a break for the N gate. Some way down the forward slope is a second ditch. Nothing is visible of the Hadrianic fortlet.

North of Birrens itself the main road through Annandale continued NW to Ladyward near Lockerbie where the road splits, one arm going N up the valley of the Annan, the other reaching W towards the Nith (below, p. 90). In 1989 a fort of *c*.2 ha. (5 acres) was located at

Ladyward through aerial reconnaissance, on a fine plateau beside the left bank of the Dryfe Water close to its confluence with the Annan, and *c.*600 m W of a long-known camp at Torwood. Multiple ditches suggest more than a single phase of occupation. (To reach Ladyward, take the A709 out of Lockerbie, turn right at a crossroads signposted Millhousebridge; at a T-junction, go left, then soon right to reach Ladyward farm. The most impressive view of the fort platform is from the SW.) The camp at Torwood, of *c.*20.4 ha. (50.4 acres) was first recorded by General Roy in the mid-eighteenth century. (Return to the T-junction, go straight ahead (eastwards) to reach the hamlet of Johnsfield. Look for a track on the right, opposite the 'woodland walk' signpost. The W defensive ditch of the camp is in line with a field boundary on the left of the track, beyond some new cottages, though nettles and thistles are currently a deterrent to close inspection.)

Another road seems likely to have branched off the Annandale route hereabouts, roughly following the modern B723, at first along the Dryfe Water to the White Esk at **Raeburnfoot***, where a fortlet of Antonine date (0.64 ha./1.6 acres), defended by a double ditch, and containing nine or more rectangular buildings (perhaps stores), was subsequently enclosed within a substantial outer work and single ditch (of 2.12 ha./5.2 acres), the latter partly eroded on the W side by the Esk. (At Eskdalemuir, watch for a minor road leaving the B709 just before it crosses to the W bank of the White Esk signposted Clerkhill; follow the minor road towards a farmhouse, then veer sharp left behind a wood, and follow the track for 1.3 km to Raeburnfoot farm.) The outlines of the fort can be seen on raised ground to the left of the farm buildings. First the visitor will cross the ditch and bank of the outer enclosure, then the ditches and rampart of the fort itself, which are particularly impressive on the S and N sides where the ditch is l m deep (Fig. 48).

The Roman road beyond Raeburnfoot to the NE can be followed on the ground to the Borthwick Water, a tributary of the Teviot. (Drive beyond Raeburnfoot farm to Mid Raeburn; stop at a gate just before a bridge leading to the farm, pass through it and follow a track along the edge of some forestry; the Roman road from Raeburnfoot crosses this track from right to left at a firebreak, and continues uphill. The low mound of the road can now be followed along the firebreak for 6 km over a sequence of hilltops, finally to reach Craik Cross Hill on the Dumfriesshire/Roxburghshire border, from which fine views are to be had on a clear day towards the Eildon Hills above Melrose.)

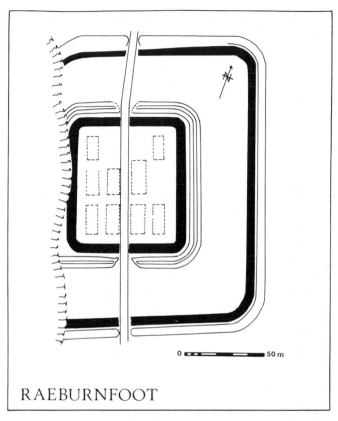

RAEBURNFOOT

48. **Raeburnfoot, Dumfries & Galloway:** ground-plan of the Antonine fort and outer enclosure (after Robertson).

The Roman road survives as a low mound, sometimes with cuttings to ease the gradients. On the summit of **Craik Cross Hill**, immediately N of the Roman road, and just before a boundary fence, is a circular mound, perhaps to be identified as a Roman watch-tower. (A full day is necessary for the walk from Raeburnfoot and back; the site can also be reached from the NE, from Craik village; see OS 1:50,000 sheet for details of route.) Limited excavation at the site in 1946 identified a turf-built rampart and single ditch, but no foundations for internal buildings were noted, nor were any small finds recovered, so that the Roman dating is not secure. Further NE along this road, at Milsington, on the Borthwick Water, one leg of a bronze statue, evidently of a man on horseback, perhaps loot from some fort or a town in the south, was found in 1820. A possible watch-tower at Ewes Doors, near the headwaters of the Teviot, originally interpreted as a Bronze Age round cairn, has a causeway across the defences to an adjacent road; but how this site can relate to the Roman road system as we know it is as yet unclear.

The Annandale road itself continued N along the E bank of the river. At **Dalmakethar** E of Johnstonebridge, on high ground with good views along the river valley, is a square enclosure, possibly but not certainly a Roman fortlet, with a single entrance facing the Roman road. (Take the B7076 from Lockerbie, on the alignment of the old A74; turn right at Dinwoodie Lodge onto a minor road signposted Newton Wamphray; after a crossroads and *c.*400 m after the secondary track to Dalmakethar farm, park on the left and walk uphill, on the left of the road, until the ridge is reached.) The ramparts stand to a height of l m. The results of excavation in 1939 were inconclusive as to the date and function of the site.

At **Milton** 8 km further N there was a notable complex of Roman sites originally surveyed by General Roy in the mid-eighteenth century and excavated between 1938 and 1950. Here, at the N edge of a prominent ridge overlooking the River Annan, was a fort of the Flavian period (2.79 ha./6.9 acres) overlying a native enclosure. This was replaced in the Antonine period by a fortlet placed a little to the S. (Turn left off the motorway on the A701 to Dumfries; after 2 km take the B 7076 signposted to Johnstonebridge and immediately left on to a minor road which passes below the motorway and the railway. After *c.*1 km Milton farm appears on the left. Ask there for permission to proceed, and drive through the farm to a gate across the track. Park here and follow a fence line to the left uphill to the top of the ridge. Look left to see the upstanding remains of the Antonine fortlet (see Fig. 22) whose rampart survives to a height of 1.2 m within an enclosing ditch.) North of Milton there are three camps and a possible fortlet at Beattock village. Evidently there was a staging post here for traffic before it began ascending to Beattock Summit; we could also suspect some Roman movement eastwards from Beattock towards the Ettrick Water. To the N of Beattock the Roman road rises over moorland, with accompanying quarrypits; worthwhile stretches can be viewed at Gilbert's Rig, N of Moffat.

As the road continues to rise, there is a probable watch-tower close by its course at **White Type**. (On the A701 N of Moffat, park at Auldhousehill bridge, beside a two-storeyed concrete building; go left through a farm gate 300 m ahead (the fence is electrified). Some 80 m into the field, the Roman road crosses the track going half-right towards a cutting. Follow the Roman road as it rises to reach a tiny stream, all but dry in summer; ignore a modern track, one of many hereabouts, going off to the right; continue straight ahead and after the road passes through a cutting, the watch-tower occupies a hillock on the left, just clear of forestry, with splendid views especially to the S, its shallow circular ditch interrupted by a causeway towards the road.) Further N beside the A701 a circular stone monument, a poignant memorial to a mail-coach driver and guard who in 1831 lost their lives here in the snow, serves to emphasise the bleakness and remoteness of the route, amid brooding hills in the vicinity of the 'Devil's Beef Tub'.

The construction of the final phases of the M74 motorway has brought great disruption to the local road network in the Beattock area. The new highway joins the former A74 trunk road, the nineteenth century railway, eighteenth century roads and the Roman road in jockeying for position in a narrow defile as the ground rises towards Beattock Summit to cross the watershed between the Annan and the Clyde. One result of this construction work has been the loss of part of a camp at Barnhill, east of Beattock Village, a stretch of Roman road at Paddy's Rickle Bridge, and changes in methods of access to several sites.

On the Roman road 3.5 km beyond White Type is a fortlet, at **Redshaw Burn***, first seen from the air in 1939, close to the watershed between the valleys of the Annan, Clyde and Tweed. (With the severing by the M74 motorway of the traditional access route, the site is best reached from the A701 beyond White Type; just N of the county boundary signs, and close to the farther limit of the forestry, a track leads W, signposted Nether Howcleuch [*sic*], a walk of *c*.1.5 km, to the fortlet, sitting between two branches of the Redshaw Burn. The visitor would be well advised to study an up-to-date large-scale OS map before setting out.) The fortlet, which measures *c*.20 m E–W by 17.5 m N–S, is enclosed by a rampart and by a double ditch. On the N side of the fortlet facing the road was a single gate, defended by a long stretch of ditch enclosing a small annexe. The Roman road, passing in front of the fortlet, lies just clear of the forestry. Some 3.5 km N is another watch-tower, named Beattock Summit, on a steep slope beside the Roman road; first seen from the air, it was established as

Roman in 1966. The circular ditch and external bank once stood out clearly, but the site is now destroyed by afforestation. It is clear that close surveillance was maintained along this particularly difficult stretch of road.

A further 500 m N at **Little Clyde** farm are the defences of a well-preserved marching camp of 12.7 ha. (31 acres) immediately beside the Roman road. The farm sits in the middle of the camp whose ramparts stand to a height of up to 0.7 m. (The visitor needs to continue N past the site on the motorway till he reaches the exit for the A702 to Elvanfoot, then to turn on to the B7076 signposted 'Beattock', following the new motorway S to a signpost for Little Clyde farm.) Go uphill for 30 m behind the farm, keeping to the left of a turbulent stream, to see the camp's N rampart, which can be followed both W and E for 200 m to the NW and NE corners. In the late eighteenth century a marble head of a Roman emperor or general, slightly larger than lifesize, broken off a statue, was found at Hawkshaw, close to the source of the Tweed, 10 km NE from Little Clyde; it may have been loot from a Roman site.

Nithsdale

An alternative route for the Romans (and for the modern traveller) from Carlisle to the Clyde and west-central Scotland was via the valley of the Nith. This road left the Annandale route at Ladyward (above, p. 86), and made for **Dalswinton**, where there was a large fort of the Flavian era, excavated in 1939 and shown to have an area of about 4.16 ha. (10.3 acres) over the ramparts, with accommodation for a cavalry unit. (From the A76 go south at Auldgirth onto a minor road, signposted to Dalswinton; after 3 km, at the beginning of the hamlet, turn SW on a minor road to cross the low-lying ground, noticing a dip in the slope opposite: this marks the N defences of the fort close to the NE corner (Fig. 49). Park where the road splits; the T-junction lies approximately on the site of the E gate of the fort.) There were in fact two forts at Dalswinton: the second, which was the larger of the two, occupies low ground beside the Nith at Bankfoot farm; it seems likely to have been the earlier, and may belong to the period of Agricola's active campaigning. Other Roman camps and installations in the Dalswinton area, including a watch-tower, have been tentatively identified from the air.

In the Antonine period, Dalswinton was replaced as the likely

49. **Dalswinton, Dumfries & Galloway:** the Antonine fort seen from the N (Photo: RCAHMS, Crown copyright).

nodal point of Roman activity in Nithsdale by a new fort at **Carzield**, 5 km to the S. (Continue S from Dalswinton on the minor road, then sharp right at a cream-painted cottage; park in the middle of the hamlet at the lodge-house, which is almost at the centre of the fort (Fig. 51). The visitor can walk either E or S to view the limits of the fort-platform, with some hints of the defences beyond, which enclosed an area of 2.95 ha. (7.3 acres). The modern roads still pass out of the fort more or less on the sites of the four gateways. A stone-built cavalry barracks, excavated in 1939, is marked today by a long mound in the SE quarter of the fort. W of the fort, the ground drops away steeply to the floodplain of the Nith. Finds from some of the fort's rubbish-pits, dug out in 1967–68, are in Dumfries Museum.

Northwards from Carzield, the Roman road, here followed by the modern A76, was protected in the Antonine period by a fortlet at Barburgh Mill on a high plateau above the east bank of the Nith (Fig. 22). The site is now quarried away, but comprehensive excavation in 1971 revealed two timber-framed buildings, sufficient

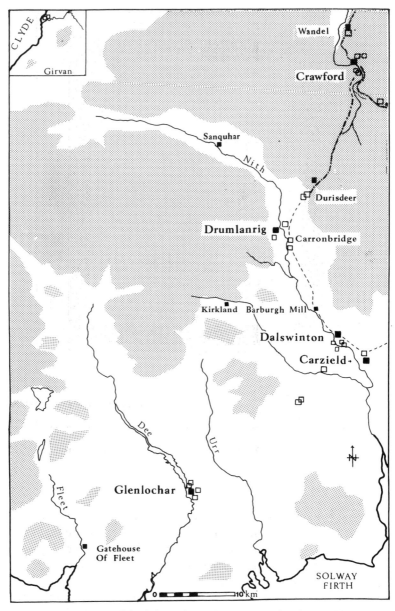

50. **Nithsdale and South-West Scotland.**

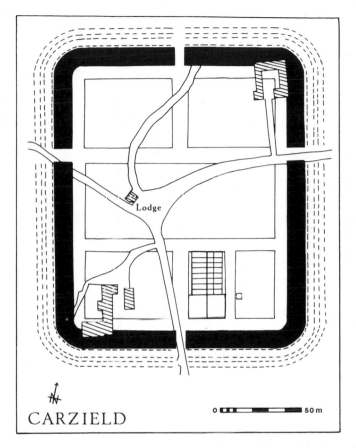

CARZIELD

51. **Carzield, Dumfries & Galloway:** ground-plan of Antonine fort (after Birley and Richmond).

to house a century of 80 men, perhaps outstationed from Carzield. At Carronbridge aerial photography long ago revealed a complex of sites, including a temporary camp, but other features are better placed in the Iron Age or medieval periods. Part of the site was explored in 1989 in advance of roadbuilding.

In the summer of 1984 a small fort of some 1.5 ha. (3.7 acres) was found from the air on the other, W, side of the Nith at Drumlanrig (The Castle here is signposted from the A76; follow the splendid driveway towards the Castle, then at the last moment turn left to a 'plant centre'). The fort-platform is easily seen on the ground; walk to the S edge of the plateau, overlooking the floodplain of the Nith. The S rampart stands to a height of 0.4 m just back from the escarpment, and the hollow of a ditch can be seen at the SW corner: an annexe has also been plotted from the air, as has a marching camp, and Antonine pottery has been found nearby, a dating confirmed by excavation in 2004. There is another camp, at Islafoot, on the far (eastern) side of the river. The Drumlanrig fort surely points to the existence of a road, its course as yet undetected, following the Nith NW towards Kilmarnock and the Ayrshire plain; a fortlet lies on this hypothetical route at Sanquhar, above the crossing of the Crawick Water. The discovery in 1989 of a fortlet at Kirkland on the Cairn Water near Moniaive could presuppose a road running SW from Carronbridge, on the line of the A702, towards the valley of the Dee, indicating a more intense surveillance of secondary valleys than we might have expected.

The known road veers away NE, and where it rises to enter the pass above the village of **Durisdeer****, there is a magnificently preserved fortlet. (Turn off the A702 4 km N of Carronbridge, along a minor road – overlying the Roman road – into Durisdeer village; park at the church (which contains a fine baroque monument to the first and second Dukes of Queensberry) and take a track on its right N for *c*.800 m; pass through a field gate on the left, and shortly after crossing a stream the fortlet should be in full view straight ahead.) The fortlet was defended by a rampart of turf now standing 1.2 m high, within a single ditch (Fig. 52). These defences present a formidable obstacle still, with a height-difference of some 4 m between the bottom of the ditch and the top of the rampart. The gate was to the NE (facing into the pass), and was defended by a traverse ditch and rampart – the former is still visible, *c*.11 m long and 0.3 m deep. Excavation in 1938 revealed the foundations for two timber buildings in the interior, and evidence of two phases of occupation. The road climbs to enter the pass, to the left of the Kirk Burn and subsequently of the Potrail Water. (A walk of 6 km, much recommended.) At first the course of the road is marked by a modern track, but where the latter peters out it can be detected by terracings as it continues uphill. (Keep to the left of the field dyke.) Joined again by a modern track, it curves left round the Well Hill, till it descends towards the modern A702. Where the Roman road approaches the modern highway (which has here followed the lower, and even more spectacular, Dalveen

52. **Durisdeer, Dumfries & Galloway:** Antonine fortlet, seen from the NE, looking down into the valley of the Nith (Photo: L. Keppie).

Pass), it survives as a fine cambered mound, which continues across the modern road for 500 m before veering right and descending towards Overfingland, where stretches are visible left of the modern highway before and after the farm. The Roman road now ran on NE; its course may be detected from time to time N of the line of the A702, especially between Glenochar and Elvanfoot. At Air Cleuch on this route, beyond Glenochar, stones which may have constituted a bridge abutment are visible beside a stream bed. (Look for a low bridge parapet on the left side of the modern road, almost opposite farm buildings in fields to the right; walk uphill from here for 250 m). The Roman road eventually joined the Annandale route at Crawford (below, p. 96).

Roman incursions along the Scottish coastline of the Solway Firth, or perhaps incursions up the river valleys from the Firth, are demonstrated by a camp on either side of the mouth of the River Annan and another further W at Ruthwell (Fig. 44). Close by the mouth of the Nith, a fort at **Ward Law** bestrides a saddleback ridge which stands out from afar. (Off the B725 S of Dumfries close to Caerlaverock Castle. Best reached from a rough farm-track going uphill opposite a sign for a Wetlands Centre; continue uphill behind the farm, keeping to the right of a circular plantation of trees at the

S end of the ridge.) The climb is very worthwhile for views over the Solway, but the ramparts may prove difficult to detect if the crop is high; the fort's E rampart can be seen as a dip in the field about two-thirds up the slope. Excavation in 1939 and 1949–50 revealed that the fort had an area of 2.8 ha. (6.9 acres); the single enclosing ditch was partly rock-cut. No small finds were made, so that the date of the fort is uncertain. Its large size may argue for the Flavian period. The trees at the end of the ridge conceal the double ramparts of an Iron Age hillfort, to which the Roman fort was apparently linked by a ditch. On lower ground to the SW, immediately behind the sand-flats at the mouth of the Nith, is a likely fortlet, at Lantonside, located from the air.

A route SW from Dalswinton led towards a major concentration of installations at **Glenlochar** on the Kirkcudbrightshire Dee, immediately S of Loch Ken, where a large fort of some 3.36 ha. (8.3 acres), occupied in both Flavian and Antonine periods, is hedged about with at least five camps. Obviously, substantial Roman forces passed this way on several occasions. (On the A713, 3 km N of Castle Douglas, turn left on to the B795; the fort lies at a group of cottages just before the river.) The fort-platform can be made out, and the W rampart (on the left of the road just beyond the cottages) survives as a low mound 0.3 m high with a causeway across the ditches (Fig. 39). At Gatehouse of Fleet, a fortlet was located from the air in 1949, and excavated in 1960–61. It lay on high ground overlooking the course of the Water of Fleet, with good views N up the river valley. It is difficult to suppose that this was the terminal site for any Roman road along the coast of Galloway, and indeed further stretches have been identified along the coast, together with a marching camp at Glenluce. Undoubtedly permanent installations also await discovery, for example at Newton Stewart and at or near Stranraer, where Loch Ryan provides a fine natural harbour. A burial cairn at High Torrs on the Luce Sands, Wigtownshire, was found in 1931 to contain grave-goods including an onyx finger ring, iron objects and second/third century pottery. Other Roman material has been been recovered from Luce Sands over many years.

Clydesdale

At **Crawford** village, now bypassed by the M74, a small fort, placed at the confluence between the River Clyde and the Camps Water,

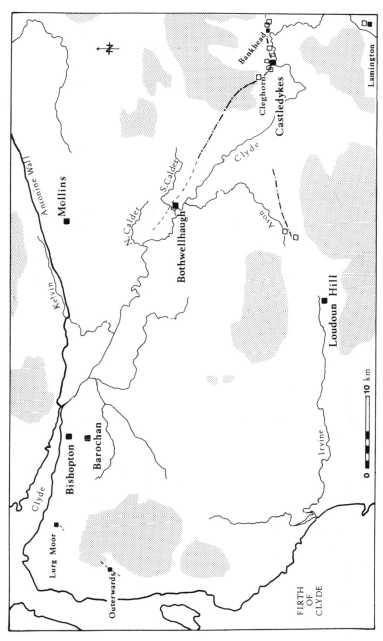

53. The Clyde Valley.

marked the junction between the Annandale and the Nithsdale Roman roads. Initially discovered from the air in 1938 and confirmed as Roman by trial excavation, the fort was extensively excavated in 1961–66 when occupation was demonstrated in both Flavian and Antonine periods, when it was enlarged to 1.06 ha. (2.6 acres), with ramparts of turf and internal buildings of timber. (Turn off the M74 on the A702 for Crawford village; at the N end of the main street, turn right at a monument to cross the railway, immediately left then right once more at a T-junction; park at or before a cottage on the right near the ruins of Castle Crawford. The fort lies in the field opposite.) Little can be made out except that the N and W ramparts may be vaguely discernible in pasture, as are the SW, NW and NE corners. Go to the second pair of trees, directly opposite the cottage, to see the line of the W rampart. At Crawford the Roman road left the valley of the Clyde, to climb through the hills E of the river, on a more direct route towards Abington than that followed today by the M74. (From the fort, head towards the hills, then go right, along the fence, to a group of trees. Now go uphill for 400 m. The alignment may prove difficult to detect.) The road soon passes through a cutting, and turns sharp right to follow a level terrace, becoming more and more impressive as it works its way round the lower slope of **Raggengill Hill**; it can now be followed easily for 1.5 km, though the course is occasionally interrupted by the metalled track of an eighteenth-century successor. The road continues towards Abington with the Raggengill Burn below, and the ramparts of an impressive Iron Age fort on Arbory Hill above. At Wandel, 4 km N of Abington, are a probable fortlet (similar in size to Redshaw Burn) and a temporary camp. At nearby Lamington a camp has been observed together with another possible fortlet. The Roman road continued NE past Biggar, crossing the Tweeddale road (below, p. 118) at Melbourne (where the A702 from the S still crosses the A721), and continued NE along the S flank of the Pentlands, and latterly along the left bank of the North Esk, heading for the River Forth at Inveresk (below, pp. 123). Surprisingly there is as yet no direct link confirmed from Crawford (or Lamington) to the important fort at Castledykes (below), for example along the Clyde itself past Thankerton on the line of the A73 and the railway, though such a route is reported by the antiquarian writers.

The fort at **Castledykes** is situated above the Clyde where the hills have opened out to leave a wide stretch of flat land fringed by the western Pentlands and Tinto Hill. (On the A70 E of Lanark;

3 km N of Hyndford Bridge, turn right at a line of houses; follow the farm-track signposted to Corbiehall, and, where the road bends to the left at a bungalow, go straight on; after 200 m the rising ground marks the beginning of the fort-platform.) The limits of the fort, which had an area of 3.2 ha. (7.8 acres), are easily made out on all sides, especially on the S where the ground drops away towards the floodplain of the Clyde. (It should be remembered that the course of the Clyde has changed over the centuries and that in Roman times it probably flowed closer to the fort.) The track passes through the fort's W gate on a slight causeway, with the ditch visible to either side and as a matching hollow in the nearby field-fence to the S. Continue on the track, through another gate, beyond which a substantial mound, standing on either side of the track to a height of 1.5 m, represents the E rampart (Fig. 54). Excavation between 1937 and 1955 established that the fort, which faced S towards the Clyde, was occupied in both the Flavian and Antonine periods. The central buildings were probably of timber in the Flavian period but certainly of stone in the Antonine; a squared building-block, having one face dressed to receive an inscription, and decorated with the incised figure of a capricorn, testifies to construction work by men of the Second Legion,

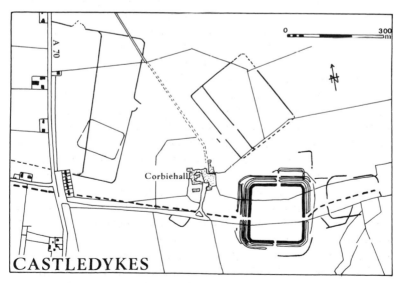

54. **Castledykes, South Lanark:** ground-plan of the fort and nearby marching camps (after RCAHMS).

which used the capricorn as one of its emblems. A lead-sealing found by metaldetecting in the 1990s bears the name of the *ala Sebosiana*, a cavalry regiment, perhaps its garrison in the Antonine period. To the N and W of the fort were half a dozen temporary camps, revealed by aerial photography, for troops in transit. Clearly this was an important staging post, as was its nearby Victorian equivalent, Carstairs railway junction.

What seems to be the course of a Roman road running NW into Clydesdale can be seen just W of Castledykes fort, where it survives in a narrow strip of woodland N of the farm access road. Soon after, the road passes a well-preserved camp of 17.75 ha. (43.8 acres) at **Cleghorn*** surveyed by William Roy in 1764, parts of whose N and E sides survive impressively in a forestry plantation, though now heavily overgrown. (Best reached from the A706 out of Lanark; soon after a level-crossing, take an unsignposted minor road N opposite a new house towards some woodland; look for the driveway to another new house on higher ground to the left. From this point walk back 20 m to a telegraph pole on the opposite (N) side of the road. (Or walk forward to it from a parking place on the right of the road.) This pole sits in line with the camp's N rampart which can be seen extending into the plantation, called Camp Wood.) The rampart may be followed on foot for 350 m to its NE corner, with the ditch on the left, now serving as a drainage channel (Fig. 55). At the corner, the rampart turns sharply to the right and can be followed with increasing difficulty (modern plantation bankings confuse the Roman line) towards the A706. There were two entrances in the N side of the camp, both marked by traverses lying 10 m beyond the rampart. The first lies just 40 m into the plantation beyond the minor road; it can be reached by the intrepid visitor. The second lies 150 m further on.

The Roman road now continues NW well above the right bank of the Clyde. The best visible stretch is at **Collielaw Wood**. (Continue along the minor road N from Cleghorn past woodland on the left; just short of Collielaw farm, walk left along the line of a double wire fence on the N side of the woodland, almost to the far edge of the wood, where a cambered mound with side-ditches comes into view.) Its course is visible running both N towards Collielaw farm and S into the wood. Excavation has confirmed the presence of a metalled road scarcely 5 cm below the modern surface; but this may represent resurfacing of the Roman road during the eighteenth century. The road continues N on high ground until it is swallowed up in the

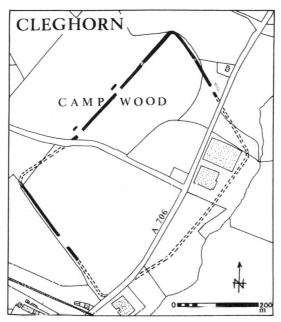

55. **Cleghorn, South Lanark:** ground-plan of the marching camp (after RCAHMS).

modern towns of Wishaw and Motherwell, where its alignment is preserved for a while by the modern A721.

North of Motherwell, within the grounds of Strathclyde Country Park, on high ground above the (former) junction between the Clyde and the South Calder Water, there was a fort of 1.65 ha. (4 acres) known today as **Bothwellhaugh***. (From the M74, take the exit to Motherwell, A723, or the exit to Bothwell, A725; look for signs to Strathclyde Country Park. Within the Park, drive to the modern bridge across a small river, the South Calder Water. Park off the road in a picnic area S of the river, at the top of the slope; the fort-site lies immediately to the N.) First reported in the 1790s, the fort was excavated in 1938–39 and in 1967–68 (Fig. 56). Only the SE rampart can be detected with some difficulty in wooded ground immediately N of the picnic area, where it stands to a height of up to 1.2 m; the modern footpath leading downhill almost immediately crosses the fort's SE corner, with the embankment on the right representing what remains of the fort's NE rampart; other stretches of the fort's

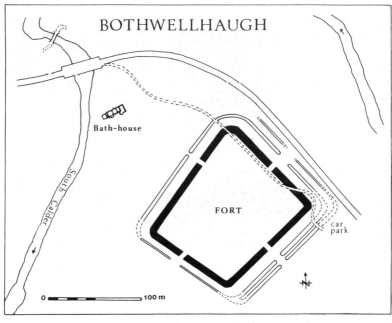

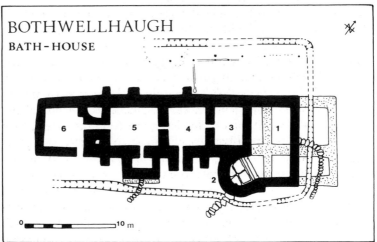

56. **Bothwellhaugh, North Lanark.** Top: fort and bath-house (after RCAHMS). Bottom: bath-house (after Keppie). Note: 1 = cold room, 2 = cold plunge bath, 3–4 = warm rooms, 5 = hot room, 6 = main furnace. Stippling indicates foundations for walling which was never completed.

57. **Bothwellhaugh**: the bath-house from the NW, looking from the furnace room towards the cold room (Photo: L. Keppie).

rampart also survive, but in the summer's high growth little can be discerned. The site offers splendid views up and down the Clyde valley. Below the fort, beside the South Calder Water, the fort bath-house was accidentally discovered in 1973 during the construction of Strathclyde Country Park, and excavated in 1975–76 in anticipation of flooding from the adjoining artificial loch, which now lies between the fort and the Clyde itself. (Continue down the footpath almost to the river.) In 1979–81 the remains were re-excavated, dismantled and rebuilt on the same site at a higher level, safe from the encroaching waters (Fig. 57). The bath-house was a finely constructed sandstone building, about 30 m by 10 m, with a cold room at the E end (nearest the fort). In the centre of the cold room floor was a slab carved with a floral design (Fig. 58), to serve as a 'drain cover' (the original slab is in the Hunterian Museum; a replica placed in situ was soon vandalised). Opening off the cold room was a semicircular cold-plunge bath (Fig. 59), and a sequence of heated rooms provided with underfloor hypocausts. At the W end of the building, adjacent to the South Calder, was a furnace room. An information board supplies useful details. Close by is an attractive hump-backed bridge, known locally as the Roman Bridge; it may have been built towards the end of the fifteenth century.

58. **Bothwellhaugh:** floral drain-cover in centre of cold-room floor of the bath-house (Photo: W.A.C. Sharp; scale in inches).

Beyond Bothwell the Roman road ran through Uddingston to Mount Vernon; some camps and even a fortlet might be looked for at the crossing of the North Calder Water, but the ground has been built over, or much disturbed. Interestingly there is a major motorway interchange nearby. The course of the road through Glasgow itself is lost. We could suppose that it was heading for the W terminus of the Antonine Wall at Old Kilpatrick or for the fort at Balmuildy on the River Kelvin (below, p. 149). On high ground at Yorkhill in Glasgow, where the Kelvin meets the Clyde, Roman material of the Antonine period, including a coin and some pottery, was found long ago, but it has usually been thought to indicate a native homestead occupied in the Roman period. But the site would be ideal for an intermediate fort or fortlet between Bothwellhaugh and Old Kilpatrick.

To the E of Glasgow, at Mollins farm close to the modern A80 (Glasgow-Stirling road) on the Luggie Water, a small fort was unexpectedly revealed from the air in 1977; it was about 0.4 ha. (1 acre) in size with an annexe to the W. Trial excavation in 1977–78

59. **Bothwellhaugh:** cold plunge bath on excavation, 1975 (Photo: L. Keppie; scale in feet).

established a Flavian date, so that Mollins may have been one of the garrison-posts which Tacitus tells us were constructed along the Forth-Clyde isthmus by Agricola in AD 80.

Another Flavian site, perhaps also to be linked to Agricola's work in AD 80, is at Barochan Hill (2 km N of Houston in Renfrewshire, within a private estate). The fort was first seen from the air in 1953; excavation in 1972 and in 1984–86 established the position of two gateways and the alignment of internal buildings. The fort, of about 1.4 ha. (3.5 acres), with an annexe to the E, had wide views in all directions, though the site lies too far S of the Clyde to have exercised direct control over movements on or across the river. In the Antonine period, Barochan was not reoccupied, but its place was taken by a 1.79 ha. (4.4 acre) fort at Bishopton, on a plateau directly overlooking the Clyde, the lowest fordable point on the river's course at Dumbuck, and (on its further bank) the hillfort on Dumbarton Rock which was certainly occupied in the early centuries AD, and later became the capital of the Dark Age British kingdom of Strathclyde. Bishopton fort was located from the air in 1949 and extensively excavated in 1950–54. Nothing meaningful is visible today, but the visitor cannot fail to be impressed by the extensive views over the Clyde estuary, with Dumbarton Rock immediately opposite and the mountains of

Argyllshire providing a backdrop. (To appreciate the fort's position, take a minor road half-left going W out of Bishopton village; after 1.5 km, beyond a new 'equestrian centre', where the road begins to descend, and the Clyde comes into view, look for a clump of trees on the N side of the road. The fort lies mainly in the field to the S.)

Close Roman surveillance over the Firth of Clyde can be assumed, with a sequence of watch-towers and fortlets along the S bank of the river. In 1952 aerial reconnaisance revealed a fortlet on **Lurg Moor*** above Greenock, with magnificent views towards the Gare Loch, the Holy Loch, and Loch Long. (In Greenock, travelling W on the A8, turn S opposite the harbour, at the fire-station, on to the B788 signposted to Kilmacolm, then after passing below the railway turn left at traffic lights into Ingleston Road, then Kilmacolm Road, amid much new housing; turn into Leven Road, then Renton Road and next Arden Road, at the end of which park in an inshot directly overlooking the Clyde. Walk up the hillside behind the houses past the line of pylons and continue uphill across heather-covered ground to the next ridge. If in doubt head for the highest point on the ridge. A cairn of small stones visible from the pylon lies just W of the fortlet. An E–W fence hereabouts lies just S of the fortlet-ditch. Allow 30 minutes for the stiff climb across marshy, gorse- and heather-covered ground.) The fortlet-rampart stands up to 0.8 m high, with a single rock-cut ditch now 0.8 m deep, interrupted by a causeway to the gate which is placed on the S side. Less certainly there is a second gate in the N rampart. There has been no excavation here, but Roman pottery found on the surface nearby was of Antonine date. A road led S from the fortlet (its cambered mound may be detectable S of the fortlet across marshy ground) along the line of the Old Largs Road, past Loch Thom.

In 1970 a similar fortlet was located on this road at **Outerwards**. (5 km S of Loch Thom, turn right on to a farm track to Outerwards farm; follow field boundaries leading uphill behind the farm buildings to reach the top of the ridge; then turn right along the spine of the ridge for *c.*300 m, till the ground begins to fall away.) The fortlet has a fine prospect over the Firth of Clyde, with panoramic views of the Cowal peninsula, Bute, the Cumbrae Islands, Arran and occasionally beyond. The near circular ditch survives to a depth of 0.5 m, with a low mound preserving some small part of the rampart-stack. There were two small buildings in the interior, located by excavation in 1970. The site is traversed by a stone-bottomed estate road. The terminal point of the Roman road could have been Largs, where a fragment of samian pottery has been found.

It need not be doubted that other forts and fortlets have yet to be located, for example along the upper reaches of the Nith towards the Water of Ayr, and along the Avon river W of Castledykes where a road is known heading due W towards Irvine. A good stretch of this road can be seen at **Dykehead** near Stonehouse. (From the A71 in the W outskirts of Stonehouse beside a school, take Sidehead Road, signposted to Avondyke Training Centre, to a junction, then left onto a minor road marked 'Kirkmuirhill 4'; at a point two field boundaries S of Dykehead farm, which lies just beyond the Training Centre, go left through a field-gate, and follow the track downhill, overlying the Roman road; in the second field the cambered mound is in view, though regrettably now actively in use as an access track.) The embankment stands 0.5 m high, and can be followed on foot for 2 km to Gil farmhouse (Fig. 25). Two camps have been identified along this route near Strathaven.

Halfway between Castledykes and Irvine Bay was a small fort, of some 1.43 ha. (3.5 acres) at Loudoun Hill, where the River Irvine passes through a defile. The fort is now lost through gravel digging, but excavation between 1938 and 1948 showed several phases of occupation in the Flavian period and renewed occupation at the very beginning of the Antonine period, when it quickly passed out of use. A timber-framed headquarters building and commanding officer's house lay alongside barracks, stables or stores and a granary. Finds (now in the Hunterian Museum) included a bronze hanging lamp and much ironwork, including wagon-wheel tyres, axle fittings, tools and spearheads. There was an annexe to the SE, defended by two ditches. The Loudoun Hill fort cannot have stood alone, and a Roman site at the mouth of the River Irvine (which could be the place named *Vindogara* by Ptolemy) has long been postulated. Tacitus tells us that Agricola placed garrisons on the coast facing Ireland: in recent years two marching camps have been found at Girvan, from one of which has come a fragment of first-century glass, suggesting that the site belongs in Agricola's time.

Redesdale and Tweeddale

For the Romans advancing N from the line of the Tyne at Corbridge (see Fig. 8) the favoured route was by way of the River Rede towards

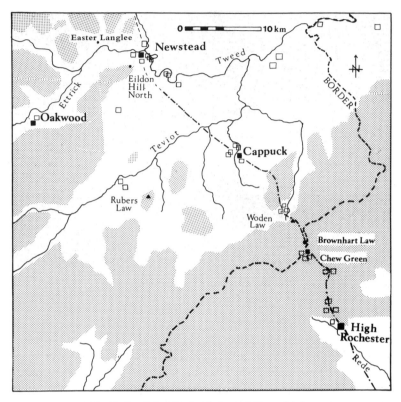

60. **Redesdale, Teviotdale and Tweeddale.**

the Tweed at Melrose, and then by the Leader Water towards the
Forth at Musselburgh. This route, known from Anglo-Saxon times
as Dere Street, is followed (for the greater part of its length) by the
line of the modern A68.

There was also a Roman road running NE from Corbridge to the
river Aln at Learchild, and then to the coast at Berwick where a fort
must surely lie undetected, but no continuation towards Edinburgh
(on the line now used by the railway and the A1) is yet known, though
isolated finds of Roman material have been plotted along the coasts
of Berwickshire and East Lothian.

The course of Dere Street in Northumberland is marked by
numerous Roman camps whose defences have survived impressively
in upland pastures. Professor Roger Wilson's authoritative *Guide to the*

61. **Chew Green, Northumberland:** aerial view looking N along Dere Street into Scotland (Photo: Cambridge University Committee for Aerial Photography).

Roman Remains in Britain notices the chief sites. Particularly worthy of a visit are forts at Risingham (near the village of West Woodburn) and at High Rochester; close to the latter is the Brigantium Archaeological Reconstruction Centre, with various outdoor mock-ups.

At **Chew Green****, N of High Rochester, just before (i.e. on the English side of) the Border, a fortlet and marching camps can be seen in a wild, almost ageless, upland setting which highlights their isolated position. (The visitor on foot may approach from the N via Pennymuir and Woden Law, starting at Tow Ford; see below for details of this route. Alternatively, direct access along Dere Street from the S to Chew Green may be possible by road from Redesdale army camp at Rochester village; but the visitor using this route must check first that firing is not in progress on adjacent military ranges. A whole day is advised for the walk from Chew Green to Pennymuir and back; and possession of the relevant OS 1:50,000 sheet is essential. Car users should also be able to utilise the more direct minor road from the A68 at the Cottonhope Road End, S of Byrness, opposite a caravan park, which can be followed past some farms to the top of a ridge, then left for 3 km to a turning-place beyond a bridge. There is a colourful information board here. The visitor should then walk uphill to the finger-post for the Pennine Way, and continue to the top of the slope, for a better view of the rather confusing complex, whose elements can be difficult to disentangle on the ground (see Figs. 61–62). An information board here would help greatly. The visitor on this convenient route may nevertheless still be turned back if military exercises are in progress.)

Occupation at Chew Green in both Flavian and Antonine periods is likely. The smallest surviving earthwork at Chew Green, but the only one of a permanent nature, is a fortlet of the Antonine period, with a prominent rampart crossed by a causeway to a gate in its NE side, and a triple ditch beyond; there are two small annexes to the E. Nearby is a temporary camp, itself lying within a second camp of 7.6 ha. (18.7 acres). The W ditch of the inner camp is particularly impressive, with a depth of 1.5 m. Another temporary camp lies to the N.

Dere Street now turns to cross a stream (the Chew Sike) and heads N. It survives as a broad flattened mound, sometimes disfigured by medieval and more modern trackways. Just 900 m N of Chew Green, and almost straddling the Border, is a small fortlet at Brownhart Law which observed movement along the Roman road, here closely followed by the Pennine Way; users of the latter, hikers bent against wind and rain, pay the almost invisible Roman site little attention. The low heather-covered rampart of the fortlet, now standing 0.45 m high, is enclosed by a double ditch, with a single opening on the E side towards the road. (The site lies close to the fence marking the Border, to the left of the Pennine Way, shortly after the fence, descending from a summit to the left, turns sharply N; beside the Roman road is a large quarry pit.)

The Roman road can now be followed N from Brownhart Law over wild moorland, where it survives as a substantial cambered mound, round the N side of Blackhall Hill (the OS 1:50,000 sheet shows a separate pathway running S of this hill) towards **Woden Law**, whose summit is enclosed by the rampart and triple ditches of an Iron Age fort. A little way below them, on the S and E flanks of the hill, are outerworks comprising a triple ditch curving round the hillside, and (further down) a double ditch running N–S which cuts another double ditch. Some have believed these outerworks to represent siegeworks, or practice-works of Roman date; but they may be defensive dykes to be associated with the hillfort itself. The Roman road makes its way round the E side of Woden Law, and descends to cross the Kale Water at **Pennymuir****, where a group of four camps sits to either side of the road. (Car users should leave the A68 at the sign for Edgerston Tofts; after 6 km take the minor road signposted Hownam; a further 2 km brings the visitor to a T-junction at a smart red-roofed wooden building. Dere Street underlies the road running S from this point towards the Kale Water at Tow Ford; look here for a farm gate and stile on the right, after 300 m.) Lying parallel to the modern road, some distance within the field on the right, are the E defences of the largest camp, of 17 ha. (42 acres); in line with the modern gate is one of its gateways, protected by a traverse. Modern bankings continuing the Roman alignments may confuse the visitor. Later, a smaller camp was set into the SE corner of the larger, utilising parts of the existing defences. (Now walk forwards, at right angles to Dere Street; this line represents the N side of the smaller camp. Continue past a traverse protecting the N gate of the smaller camp, across the interior of the large camp, whose centre is disfigured by a forestry plantation, to its far (W) side, which is reached at another gateway with protecting traverse. The long course of its W rampart (standing 1 m high) and the ditch marked by a line of reeds stand out clearly in winter, even better in snow. Turn right and follow the rampart of the large camp to its NW corner and then along the N side, back to the access road.) Two other camps are known at Pennymuir, on the other side of Dere Street: the SW corner of one of these lies just opposite the NE corner of the larger camp just described; the fourth camp lies a little to the S.

Dere Street can be followed N on foot from Pennymuir, but recent damage by bikers and off-road vehicles is reprehensible. (Walk back from Pennymuir camps to the wooden building, then follow a track going directly forward for 5 km to **Whitton Edge**, where it briefly survives as a substantial mound flanked by quarry pits; also reached direct from Jedburgh via Oxnam; watch for a cattle grid on the spine of the ridge.) Thereafter the road dips to cross the Oxnam Water where a small fort at Cappuck was first investigated in 1886 and further excavated in 1911. There are no meaningful surface traces of the fort today, but the line of Dere Street is visible both N and S of the fort. (The road, helpfully signposted, can be followed on foot from Whitton Edge past Cappuck to the River Teviot, opposite Monteviot House, where a fort has been sought, so far without success; most of the route is unsuitable for cars.) A fragment of a

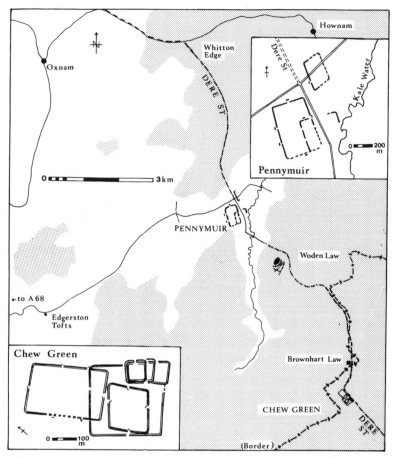

62. **Dere Street,** from the Scottish Border to Whitton Edge; insets: Pennymuir and Chew Green.

finely sculptured slab bearing the boar-emblem of the Twentieth Legion was recovered from Cappuck in 1886; it is now in the Museum of Scotland, Edinburgh.

At Jedburgh 5 km to the W of Cappuck are parts of two inscribed Roman altars reused as building material in the twelfth-century Abbey. One is now a lintel stone, at the entrance to the North Stair of the Abbey. (The stone, dedicated to Jupiter by a detachment of spearmen under their tribune Julius Severus, is above your head as you pass through the wooden door leading to the stair.) The

63. **Eildon Hills, Scottish Borders**, from the SE under snow: Roman *Trimontum* (Photo: L. Keppie)

other, erected by the First Cohort of Vardullians under their tribune C. Quintius Severus, served as a paving slab at the NE corner of the Presbytery; it is now on view at the Visitor Centre. From the information they bear, the two altars belong best in the early third century AD and may form evidence of Severan reoccupation at nearby Cappuck, but they could alternatively have been carried northwards from the forts at High Rochester or Risingham by the builders of the Abbey. Built into the S wall of the Undercroft of the Abbey, near its W end, is a roughly squared-off fragment of what could be a third Roman altar, on which some uncertain, perhaps floral, motifs can be discerned.

North of Cappuck, the road runs straight for the Eildon Hills beside the Tweed. Any doubts about the equation between the Eildons and the Latin placename *Trimontium*, reported by Ptolemy and attested in documentary sources, will be removed when the walker coming from the south on Dere Street, well preserved here, tops the rise on Ancrum Moor, at 'Lady Lilliard's Stone' and surveys the 'triple peaks' straight

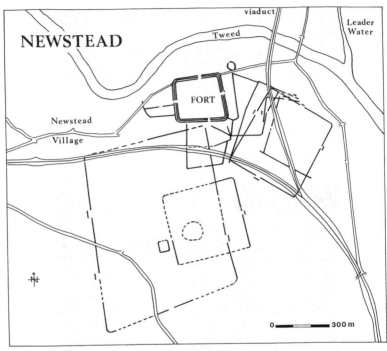

64. **Newstead, Scottish Borders:** fort and nearby marching camps (after RCAHMS, with additions); a further camp has been identified from the air to the E, at Broomhill.

ahead (Fig. 63). At **Newstead**, a village on the E fringe of Melrose, a major complex of Roman sites (Fig. 64) has been revealed over the years. (From the A68, turn left, before the line of the Tweed, on to the A6091, then right into Newstead village (fort signposted). Near the Health Board (NHS Borders) offices at the E end of the village stands a 'Millennium Milestone', erected in 2000, and a covered information panel. The visitor should proceed E on foot, along the former B6361 until, *c.*500 m beyond the village, where the road stands high above the Tweed and a railway viaduct comes into view, a replica Roman altar stands on the right-hand verge, erected in 1928 close to the fort's NW corner; it was repainted and rededicated in 1997.) There are raised viewing platforms and information panels at regular intervals beside the modern road. Recently a length of timber breastwork has been constructed, facing the fort, with a timber tower above, on the railway

65. **Newstead, Scottish Borders:** aerial view of site from the W, with Leaderfoot viaduct visible at top left (Photo: Dr. Colin Martin).

embankment S of the river. (The fort site can also be accessed on foot directly from the A68; look for the signpost 'Leaderfoot Viewpoint'; parking is available.)

Newstead fort, the largest known permanent Roman site in Scotland apart from the legionary fortresses at Inchtuthil and Carpow, lay immediately above a crossing of the Tweed, in the shadow of the Eildons (Fig. 65). The site was excavated between 1905 and 1910, and the resulting report by James Curle, *A Roman Frontier Post and its People* (Glasgow, 1911), has become a classic, and is now a book-collectors' item; the text can also now be accessed online.

A fresh programme of geophysical survey and excavation from 1986 onwards by a team from the University of Bradford considerably

66. **Bronze face-masks from cavalrymen's helmets,** from Newstead. Highly decorated helmets were worn on special parades (Photo: National Museums of Scotland).

enhanced our knowledge of vicissitudes in the lifetime of the fort, and our awareness of industrial activities both in the extensive annexes and, for a time, in the W half of the fort interior. A possible amphitheatre has been identified on sloping ground just outside the NE corner of the fort. In 1994 the long-disused railway cutting which bisects the complex from west to east was widened and brought back into use as part of the Melrose Bypass (now the A6091). The Trimontium Trust, established in 1987 partly in response to the threat posed by the new road, successfully raised the profile of the site, both nationally and internationally, and its energies know no bounds. The Trust organises frequent events locally, and regular 'Roman walks' are led by experienced members.

Little of the fort at Newstead is to be seen on the ground today, beyond the flattened-out platform where the fort once stood, and faint traces of ditch hollows. The rich assemblage of finds has included parade-helmets (Fig. 66), metalwork and jewellery, which form an important part of the 'Early Peoples' gallery at the Museum of Scotland in Edinburgh. The charming museum in Market Square, Melrose, operated by the Trimontium Museum Trust, complements a visit to the site itself, and should ideally precede it. Some finds from the 1905–10 excavations retained locally are on view in a ground floor room of the Commendator's House at Melrose Abbey.

The fort itself, which faced E (towards the mouth of the Tweed), with its N side protected by a sharp drop to the river, was initially of 4.3 ha. (10.6 acres), though subsequently enlarged to 6 ha. (14.7 acres); it was occupied in both Flavian and Antonine periods, and probably continued in use until about AD 180, if not later. The recent discovery during fieldwalking of a fine intaglio (on view in the museum in Market Square) showing Caracalla, the elder son and successor of the Emperor Septimius Severus, could suggest that the site was again in use at the time of Severus' campaigns of AD 208–211. A detachment of the Twentieth Legion was in garrison during the Antonine period, and an altar testifies to the presence of a regiment of cavalry, the *ala Vocontiorum* originally recruited in southern France. A newly refurbished summerhouse built in the early years of the twentieth century in the grounds of the former St Andrew's College, Drygrange, now a nursing home called Grange Hall, *c*.1 km NE of Newstead, just N of the river, incorporates stonework from the fort. In the mid-1980s a small marble torso of a Roman god, presumably an offering at a shrine, was recovered from the nearby Leader Water.

The importance of Newstead as a staging post is confirmed by the presence of at least eight camps on the banks of the Tweed between the fort itself and Maxton. One camp, of 65 ha. (165 acres), lying SW of Newstead fort, could be considered the southernmost in a sequence of gigantic enclosures between Tweed and Forth, which seem likely to belong in the Severan age (above, Fig. 9).

A Roman inscribed stone recording building activity by the Twenty-Second Legion is set into a garden wall at Abbotsford House, the one-time home of Sir Walter Scott, signposted from Galashiels; it may have come originally from Falkirk. Other sculptured stones walled up in the garden were brought there from a Roman fort at Old Penrith. A small inscribed altar, unprovenanced and perhaps deriving from continental Europe, sits on the mantelpiece in the entrance hall of the House. At Easter Langlee on the E outskirts of Galashiels a stone building, perhaps a shrine, was found during quarrying in 1965; some inscribed building-stones were rescued, but full recording of the site was not possible. Some of the stones are held in the Museum of Scotland, Edinburgh; others are locally on view at the Trimontium Trust's museum in Melrose.

The hillfort on **Eildon Hill North** had been a major centre of the

Selgovae; nearly 300 circular house-platforms have been plotted in
its interior. But such intense occupation did not continue into the
Roman period, if we can deduce this from the presence on the summit
of a watch-tower, whose single enclosing ditch stands out clearly;
within its circle is a cairn of small stones. The tower, which appears
to have had a paved floor and a tiled roof, overlay a native hut. (The
summit can best be reached from the B6359 just S of Melrose, by a
minor road leading E from Dingleton, next to a golf course; beyond
the clubhouse, go straight ahead on a grassy path which will bring
the visitor on to the saddle between Eildon Mid Hill and Eildon Hill
North; then turn left to reach the latter's summit.)

East of Newstead on the lower reaches of the Tweed, aerial
reconnaissance has in recent years located several temporary camps
(see Fig. 60), presumably testimony to the progress of a task force
heading towards (or penetrating inland from) the mouth of the Tweed
at Berwick where a fort must surely have existed.

To the W of Dere Street a number of sites mark Roman penetration
into the Southern Uplands along successive river valleys. On the
summit of Rubers Law, 3 km S of Denholm village, are the defences
of a Dark Age stronghold, whose walls incorporated many shaped
stones, usually considered Roman. (The hilltop is best reached from
Denholmhill farm, off the A698.) The stones (two, with chiselling
reminiscent of Roman craftsmanship, are stored at Hawick Museum)
have been seen as evidence for a stone-built watch-tower atop the
hill, but such a structure would normally have been of timber, and
it could be that we should think rather of a permanent Roman fort
or fortlet nearby.

A fort of Flavian date (its ramparts faintly visible), in stunningly
beautiful Borders countryside, lay at Oakwood above the Ettrick
Water (of 1.8 ha./4.4 acres), with a camp nearby. Charred timbers from
the structure of the fort gateways were found in situ on excavation in
1952: one can be seen in Halliwell's House Museum, Selkirk; others
are preserved at the Museum of Scotland, Edinburgh.

At Newstead itself a road branched off Dere Street W along the
line of the Tweed, more or less on the alignment of the A72 and
subsequently the A721. Where the road veered N to follow the Lyne
Water, a concentration of permanent installations is to be found at
the village of Hallyne (7 km W of Peebles), close to the seventeenth-
century Lyne church. Firstly, in the Flavian period, a fort of 1.4 ha
(3.5 acres) was constructed S of the Lyne Water at Easter Happrew

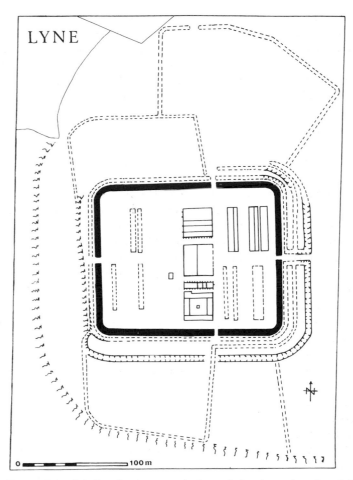

67. **Lyne, Scottish Borders**: ground-plan of the Antonine fort (after RCAHMS).

farm, with good views also to both N and S along other river valleys; nothing survives at ground level today. In the Antonine period a different (and in some ways inferior) site was chosen, on the N bank of the Lyne Water where the river made a sharp 90-degree turn (Fig. 67). The ramparts and ditches of the Antonine fort (known today as **Lyne***), which had an area of 2.66 ha. (6.6 acres), can be followed round much of the perimeter. (Park at Hallyne cottages;

walk up the lane (signposted Lyne Kirk) leading N to the church, pass through a metal farm-gate or over a stile, and turn sharp left. The plateau on which the fort lies is 200 m ahead; by aiming half-right you will first enter its E gate across a causeway.) The visible ditch is the outermost of three that originally defended the fort. Turn right to see a fragment of rampart mound at the fort's NE corner, then continue to the NW corner where a similar remnant survives. Continue down the W side of the fort to the SW corner, where a ditch splits off to enclose an annexe stretching to the escarpment above the Lyne Water. Later – but still within the Antonine period – the fort seems to have passed out of use, and a fortlet (not visible) was built just to the N with considerable views to the W along the Lyne Water itself. There are two marching camps lying a little way to the E and one to the W. West of Lyne the road headed for Castledykes. Along its course were several camps, and a fortlet at Bankhead near Carnwath.

The Lothians and Lauderdale

The existence of a road along the S flank of the Pentlands, followed now by the A702, has long been known (Fig. 68). The modern visitor who looks NE from the Clyde at Abington will immediately appreciate the significance of this route. Claims have been made from time to time for a fort at Biggar, and Alexander Gordon in 1726 referred to an enclosure 'similar to Ardoch' at Carlops. Recently a sequence of camps has been identified from the air along this route, including a site at Carlops. Parts of the NW and NE defences of a camp at North Slipperfield near West Linton, well positioned on a ridge above the Roman road, are preserved as later fencelines. A fortlet at Tocherknowe immediately NW of West Linton guarded the crossing the Lyne Water. Another camp located to the SE could suggest communication along the Lyne Water towards the Tweed.

Northwards from Newstead, Dere Street, presumably crossing the Tweed in the vicinity of the eighteenth century stone bridge, the nineteenth century Leaderfoot viaduct and the twentieth century A68, followed the Leader Water; several camps are known along its route, including one of 65 ha. (165 acres) at Channelkirk, whose once impressive ramparts are now very faint. Nearby at Oxton was a fortlet which has yielded Antonine pottery. Attached to its S side was a massive annexe, presumably to house wagons halting here overnight on this important communications artery (Fig. 69). Beyond

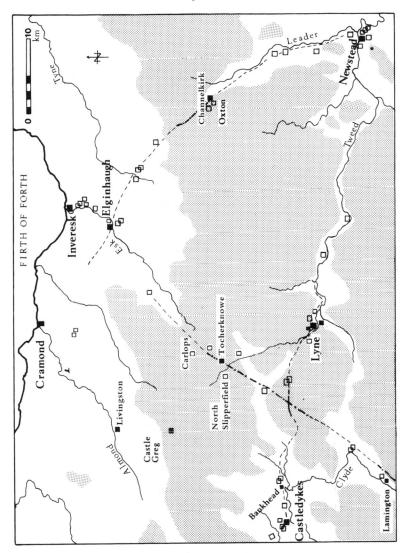

68. **Upper Tweeddale, Lauderdale and the Lothians.**

Channelkirk, Dere Street was required to negotiate a passage over Soutra, still a significant winter obstacle today, across high ground between the Lammermuirs and the Moorfoot Hills. The Roman road can be followed due N through a forestry plantation to Soutra Aisle.

69. **Oxton, Scottish Borders**: fortlet and annexes from the W (Photo: RCAHMS, Crown copyright).

(This stretch is better reached from the N, beyond the summit, by turning off the A68 on to the B6368, signposted Gilston, and parking a woodland car park just beyond the medieval hospice of **Soutra Aisle**; from the further (W) end of the wood, opposite a sign for 'Dere Street farm', walk downhill for 100 m to reach the cambered mound of the Roman road, with a large quarry pit on its uphill side. There is a small information plaque. The road may be followed further downhill, i.e. southwards, through a gap in the forestry and up the opposite slope.)

Much dressed Roman stonework, including one large block bearing the foreparts of the Pegasus emblem of the Second Legion, was found in 1869 built into a souterrain at **Crichton**, 6 km further to the NW, close to the likely line of Dere Street (Turn W off the A68 500 m N of Crichton Dean; look to the left at a gate in the third field beyond the minor road to Longfaugh farm, almost below a line of pylons. Access may be restricted if the field is in crop.) This stonework must have derived from a nearby fort, or some substantial structure, perhaps at Pathhead, where a number of camps have been detected, but no suitable installation has so far been located.

Further N the road went originally (i.e. in the Flavian period) past Eskbank (where there are two camps), to a fort on the North

Esk at Elginhaugh beside the A7 trunk road W of Dalkeith, revealed by aerial reconnaissance in 1979. Trial trenching established a Flavian date. Comprehensive excavation in 1986–87, in advance of development, revealed the complete groundplan of the fort, and part of its annexe (Fig. 19). The fort had an area of 1.4 ha. (3.4 acres); a single period of occupation in the Flavian period ended in deliberate demolition by the departing garrison. The site is now occupied by the headquarters of a Life Assurance Company. A stone bath-house on sloping ground S of the fort, identified by aerial survey, was briefly explored in 1984. From Elginhaugh the road presumably continued to the NW (probably on the line of the modern A7), perhaps making from Camelon fort (below, p. 159). Two marching camps lie more or less on this route at Gogar. A milestone of Antonine date found at Ingliston and now in the Museum of Scotland, Edinburgh, shows that the road was refurbished then (Fig. 26); part of the inscription, perhaps naming a governor of Britain later disgraced, has been erased. It is clear, however, that during the Antonine period the Elginhaugh site was replaced by a new fort nearer the Firth of Forth at **Inveresk**, on the S outskirts of Musselburgh, on high ground above a bend in the Esk close to its mouth. St Michael's Church, visible from afar, occupies part of the site and is testimony to its conspicuous position, with extensive views of the Pentland Hills, Arthur's Seat, and across the Forth to the hills of Fife. Some have detected Roman stonework incorporated into the structure of the church itself, which assumed its present form in the early nineteenth century.

Inveresk fort was investigated by Sir Ian Richmond in 1946–47, who established that it faced W and had an area of 2.84 ha.(7 acres). Something can be seen of the defences on the N side of the fort, by passing N from graveyard into the adjacent rough ground. A very substantial civil settlement stretched E from the fort, and two inscriptions indicate the presence there of an imperial procurator. Successive extensions of the graveyard and housing developments have prompted a series of excavations in recent years. Part of a hypocausted room, uncovered as long ago as 1783, with a flue leading to a furnace, and four finely-crafted cylindrical stone pillars supporting a patch of concrete flooring, can be seen in the garden of Inveresk House (Enter the grounds at a gateway almost opposite a new housing development called 'Grannus Mews' (an altar to Apollo Grannus was found hereabouts in the mid-sixteenth century, but soon destroyed as idolatrous), then request access at the house itself.) This hypocausted room could belong to the fort bath-house, though it lies nearly 300 m E of the fort itself, and may rather be part of some civilian extra-mural building. (Note that the placing of the stone pillars themselves is modern.). A curving timber-framed structure lying 900 m E of the fort has been claimed as part of a small amphitheatre, revealed by excavation in 1995.

Along the S coast of the Forth we may easily suppose a chain of posts protecting the E flank of the Antonine Wall, for example at the mouth of the Water of Leith, and further W at Hopetoun and Blackness. To date, however, only one site on the coast is known, a fort of about 2.43 ha. (6 acres) at **Cramond*** where the River Almond flows into the Forth. (Take a minor road off the A90 to Cramond at the Barnton Hotel in the W outskirts of Edinburgh; then after nearly 2 km, turn sharp left into Cramond Glebe Road. Park opposite the entrance to Cramond Kirk (a small signpost points towards the fort), or further downhill in the large public car park behind the Cramond Inn. Parts of the fort, excavated in 1954–66, are exposed to view in parkland next to the church.) A new information board offers a graphic reconstruction. Today a pleasant village, with yachts moored by the quayside, Cramond in Roman times can be envisaged as a port of some importance. Occupation in the Flavian period is uncertain, coins forming the only evidence. The known fort belongs in the Antonine age, and was refurbished at the time of Severus' campaigns. It was enclosed by a stone wall, with a clay bank behind. One wall of a stone-built workshop of Severan date has been consolidated for permanent display, and the outlines of parts of two granaries, and between them the headquarters building, together with a small latrine block in the fort's NE corner, are marked out on the ground (Fig. 70). Just beyond the latrine can be seen a length of fort rampart including the NE corner, standing to a height of 0.5 m. There is a break in the rampart mound for the E gate. Nearby are the eighteenth-century Cramond House and the restored Cramond Tower.

In 1975, the laying-out of the public car park behind the Cramond Inn brought to light a large bath-house, its walls standing up to 14 courses in height, which was backfilled through lack of funds to consolidate and display it. The bath-house lies in rough ground on the slope of the hill beside the car park (information board). The presence of a civil settlement E of the fort has been established over many years; in 2003 defensive ditches perhaps delimiting an annexe were revealed fully 300 m E of the fort, with a roadway passing through a

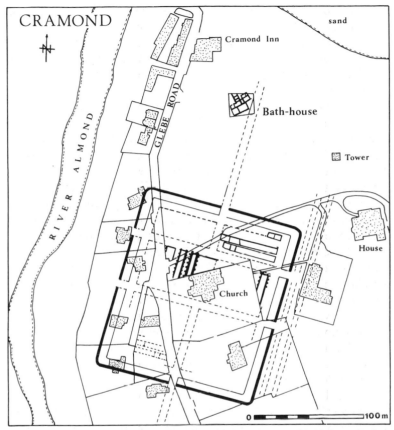

70. **Cramond, City of Edinburgh:** ground-plan of fort and bath-house (after Holmes; by courtesy of Edinburgh City Museums and Galleries).

stone-built gateway of which only foundation trenches remained. A display on the history of Cramond through the age can be seen in 'The Maltings' on weekend afternoons in the summer months.

In 1997 Cramond fort became nationally famous with the discovery of the dramatic sculpture of a lioness (see frontispiece), shown in the act of devouring her prey, the naked torso of a bearded male, which erosion of the river bank below the fort had brought to the attention of the local boatman. The lioness, and part of plinth found nearby, presumably belonged to a substantial funerary monument. It was assigned jointly to the National Museums of Scotland and Edinburgh

City Museums and is currently on view in the Museum of Scotland, in Edinburgh.

On the foreshore 500 m W of Cramond, on the far side of the River Almond, is a large rock known as **Eagle Rock**. On its E face (i.e. that facing the approaching visitor) is a sculptured figure in a niche, once interpreted as an eagle, but now better seen as Mercury (god of travel and trade) or a *Genius* (presiding spirit of the locality) holding a cornucopia and sacrificing at a little altar beside his right leg (HS plaque). The sculptural details are hard to make out. (Traditionally reached by a ferryboat service, currently discontinued; the visitor will need to divert S to Cramond Bridge and return on the opposite bank.) The Rock itself can be seen from the Cramond foreshore, with Dalmeny House in the background.

In 1992 a fortlet was plotted from the air *c.*18 km SW of Cramond, on the S bank of the River Almond, at its junction with the Killardean Burn within the new town of Livingston, opposite the old village, but whether this site is indicative of a road heading for the Clyde Valley at Bothwellhaugh or could suggest a link with the long-known fortlet at Castle Greg is not yet established.

At Linlithgow, south of Bo'ness and the E terminus of the Antonine Wall, small finds, together with aerial photography revealing defensive ditches, could suggest the presence of a Roman installation on the plateau west of the royal Palace, overlooking the adjacent loch.

At **Castle Greg***, in the empty but increasingly afforested moorland 6 km S of West Calder, is a finely preserved fortlet, with rampart and double ditch. (On the B7008 1 km N of its junction with the A70, 200 m N of a forestry plantation and 150 m E of the road.) The site stands against a fine backdrop of the Pentlands, often snowcapped in the winter months. A Flavian date is normally assigned to the site. The fortlet-rampart stands to a height of 1 m and the ditches are 2.4 m wide and 0.7 m deep. There was a single entrance on the E side. Excavation in 1852 recovered Roman pottery from a well in the centre of the fortlet. The road which this fortlet implies could have followed the N flank of the Pentlands and joined the main Clydesdale–Tweeddale route at or near the Bankhead fortlet (above, p. 120).

11
THE ANTONINE WALL

The Antonine Wall is Scotland's chief Roman monument. Much of its course of 60 kms (37 miles) between Forth and Clyde, between Bo'ness and Old Kilpatrick, can be followed in a day by car, but several days will be needed by the visitor who wishes to explore its course in detail. But while the visitor to Hadrian's Wall between Tyne and Solway has often merely to look to one side of the modern road to see stonework dramatically positioned on adjacent crags, the traveller along the Scottish frontier will not find an upstanding barrier confronting him at every point. Like a detective he must follow a trail to identify the traces of rampart-mound and ditch-hollow. These can indeed be followed for over half of the Wall's course; much remains too of the defences of the forts and fortlets placed at intervals along it.

The new frontier line was positioned on the southern side of the valleys of the River Carron and River Kelvin, with generally excellent views northwards to the ranges of hills beyond. Much the same route was followed in the 1770s by the Forth and Clyde Canal, by eighteenth century and later roads linking Edinburgh and Glasgow, and by the nineteenth century railway via Falkirk. (The more direct route between the two cities followed by the M8 motorway over higher ground via Shotts only came into regular use in the nineteenth century.)

The Antonine Wall belongs to a period of Roman history when visible barriers were being erected on several frontiers, sometimes over very long distances, to demarcate what was legally Roman from what lay beyond. In the view of some scholars these frontier works served principally as customs barriers to control but not prevent access; but the present writer views them as defensive works designed to prevent intrusion.

That the Antonine Wall frontier seems less impressive today than its Hadrianic counterpart stems largely from the materials used in its construction and the brevity of its occupation and use. The Antonine Wall was a *rampart* of laid turf, set on a stone foundation some 15 Roman feet (4.3 m) wide, with neatly dressed kerbs enclosing a rubble

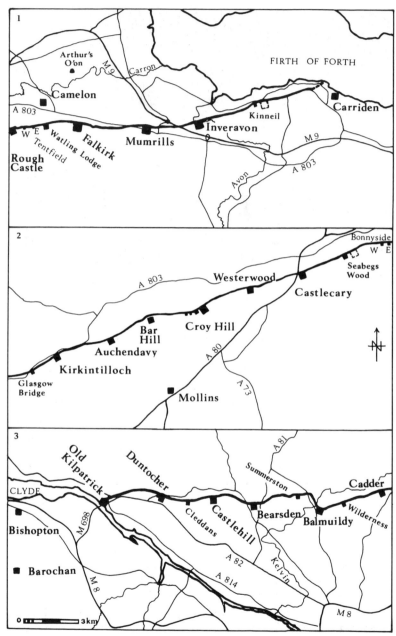

71. **The Antonine Wall:** general map showing forts, mile-fortlets and expansions along its line, from E to W.

72. **Stone rampart-base of the Antonine Wall** at Hillfoot Cemetery, Bearsden, showing culvert (Photo: L. Keppie).

core (Fig. 72). The turf superstructure, which must have attained a height of about 3.6 m, nowadays survives to a maximum height of about 1.6 m; for the most part the visitor will see no more than a low mound, and at times only a skin of turfwork may survive on top of the stone base. (A stretch of 15 km of the Wall, at the E end of the Forth–Clyde line, was in fact built not of turf but of earth held in place by narrow clay or turf cheeks.) Precisely how the rampart-stack was 'finished off' on top is not known; perhaps there was a rampart-walk, with wooden duckboards.

It is the *ditch* which has survived as the more recognisable feature today (Fig. 73). Sometimes it can be seen merely as a shallow dip in the ground along a field boundary or across a hillside; at other times, however, it presents the visitor with a formidable barrier, preserving almost its original dimensions of up to 12 m (40 feet) in breadth and 3.6 m (12 feet) in depth. It was not intended as a moat, but must on occasion, then as now, have been partly filled with water through natural drainage. Large stones, set at regular intervals, marked the edges of the ditch; the spoil was thrown out on the N side where it formed a substantial mound. In some places along its line, the berm or flat piece of ground between the Wall and the ditch, was marked by

73. **Ditch of the Antonine Wall** at Watling Lodge, Falkirk (Photo: L. Keppie).

a closely set series of oval pits, an additional defence against sudden attack. Just behind the Wall ran a road, some 6 m wide, of rough cobbles topped by gravel. This road, known today as the *Military Way*, provided a lateral communications link for the garrisons of the various forts.

Along the Wall at intervals of about 3.5 km (2 miles) were *forts*, most but not all attached to the rear of the Wall itself, which formed their N ramparts. The sites of 17 forts are securely known, and 2 more are suspected on grounds of spacing. However, it seems that when the Romans arrived on the Forth–Clyde isthmus and began the construction of the barrier, they planned to have only six forts, more widely spaced at about 14 km (8 mile) intervals (above, p. 11). The gaps

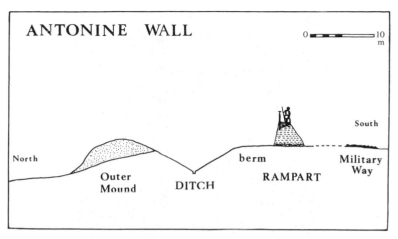

74. **Antonine Wall:** cross-section through the defences.

between them were filled by *fortlets*, attached to the Wall at roughly one-mile intervals; nine of these 'mile-fortlets' are known, and up to 30 more may await discovery. However, while the Wall was still under construction, there was a change of plan, and many more forts were added to the frontier line, to bring the total up to the 19 we know of or suspect today. Why the additional forts were built we cannot precisely say, except that a much closer surveillance of the frontier line must have been thought necessary. There are also six *expansions*, set against the back of the rampart, which may have served as signalling platforms; and near Wilderness Plantation (below, p. 149) are three *ditched enclosures* similarly placed against the S edge of the rampart, but their purpose remains unclear. In the immediate vicinity of the Wall were numerous camps (not shown on Fig. 71, but some are referred to below) which must have housed work-squads engaged on the construction of the barrier and of the forts and fortlets, but no traces of them are visible at ground level.

The precise starting point of the Wall itself on the River Forth has not so far been determined, but it seems clear that the E terminus of the frontier was protected by a fort of some 1.63 ha. (4 acres) at Carriden on the E outskirts of Bo'ness, directly overlooking the Forth. (Turn off the A904 at Muirhouses, going E on to a minor road into Carriden Estate.) The fort was found from the air in 1945, when the triple ditches forming its E defences were noted in farmland E of

Carriden House; the greater part of the fort lies within the wooded grounds of the house. In 1956 an altar to Jupiter dedicated by the residents of a village (*vicus*) beside the fort was ploughed up here, useful testimony to the existence of a civil settlement (above, p. 67; Fig. 41). The Latin inscription also gives the Roman name for the fort: *Velunia*. Aerial photography has revealed substantial traces of cultivation- and drainage-ditches nearby; to the W was an annexe defended by two ditches.

In 1868 a large distance slab was turned up on the SE slope of Bridgeness promontory, near the eighteenth-century Bridgeness Tower (built originally as a windmill), some 1.2 km W of Carriden fort; it has been generally assumed that the Wall began thereabouts, but excavation in 1985 close by the findspot of the slab failed to detect any traces of rampart or ditch. It remains possible that the Wall started further E, perhaps near Carriden itself. A modern slab inscribed with a copy of the Latin text was placed to mark the findspot of the distance slab (on the W side of Harbour Road, near the Tower), but it has suffered badly from the weather, and the Latin wording is now almost illegible.

On the high ground above Bridgeness promontory, it can be assumed that the Wall underlies Grahamsdyke Road and its westwards continuation, Dean Road (the present-day A993), after which it enters the grounds of Kinneil House, a sixteenth-century mansion with fine wall and ceiling frescoes, unfortunately now closed to the public. (As Dean Road drops away to the W, turn left into Provost Road, then immediately right.) A fort as yet unlocated could be looked for at Kinneil House. Beyond the house in an area formerly covered by a medieval village (of which only the ruined twelfth-century church now remains), the Antonine ditch can be discerned as a hollow running W in rolling farmland, now designated a Leisure Area. The Military Way too can be seen as a slight ridge running parallel to the ditch about 50 m behind it. The single tree in the field beyond sits on the N edge of the ditch.

Beyond a small reservoir the ditch can be picked up again; here on a little hilltop are displayed the remains of a mile-fortlet, originally located by trial trenching in 1978, and completely exposed for public display in 1981 (FC information board). The fortlet (named **Kinneil***) measures some 18 m E–W by some 21 m N–S, and was defended by a rampart of earth reveted by turf cheeks, set on a stone base, and by one or perhaps two ditches (Fig. 75). There were gates in the N

KINNEIL

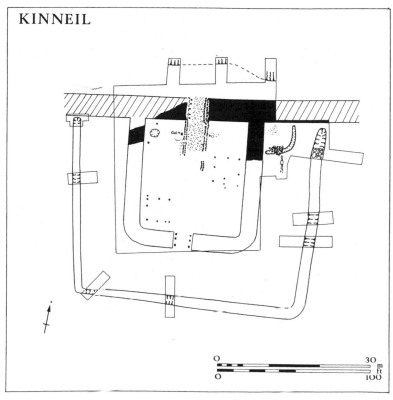

75. **Kinneil**: ground-plan of the mile-fortlet (Copyright Falkirk Museums. Reproduced by permission.

and S sides, with timber-framed towers above. The outlines of the rampart are marked on the ground by concrete slabs. The positions and layouts of the gateways and of two small buildings in the interior of the fortlet are marked by modern timbers placed in the original post-holes. A cobbled road flanked by drains ran through the fortlet from N to S. Finds from the fortlet are displayed in a nearby small museum (p. 189).

West of Kinneil the Wall follows high ground more or less on the 60 m (200 feet) contour line and overlooking the Grangemouth petrochemical complex, before descending the slope beside Inveravon Tower, a remnant of the fifteenth-century Inveravon Castle, towards the river Avon itself. A fort has long been suspected hereabouts on

...s of spacing. In 1969 some traces of walling were observed
...ial-excavation, and fieldwalking close to the river's edge has
produced flue-tiles and bricks suggestive of a bath-house. In 1990
excavation in advance of the digging of a narrow N–S pipe-trench,
one of many radiating from the nearby Grangemouth complex,
located the likely S rampart of a small fort, possibly preceded by an
'expansion', on low ground beside the Avon.

On the W bank of the Avon the ditch is clearly seen running
up the slope towards the golf-clubhouse of **Polmonthill**, but the
line of the rampart itself is now obscured by an artificial ski-slope,
which threatens to engulf this whole stretch (FC information board).
Further W, on the far side of the golf course, a fine stretch of ditch,
seldom visited today, can be seen in **Millhall Wood** (Best reached
from the B904 by turning into a car park opposite '17–19 Smiddy
Brae'; follow a path uphill straight ahead, then after 50 m veer to the
left to reach the crest of the slope; the hollow of the ditch should
now be in view; FC information board.) The Wall next rises towards
Polmont Village, where the nineteenth-century church with its twin
spires, all but overlying the frontier line, provides a useful landmark.
A long stretch of the frontier line was destroyed with the building
of the M9 motorway in the 1960s. After crossing low ground at
Beancross, the Wall now approaches the farm at Mumrills, where
there stood the largest known fort on the Wall line, some 2.8 ha.
(7 acres) in size, excavated in 1923–28 and in 1958–60. The outlines of
the fort (roughly bounded by Beancross Road, Sandy Loan and the
A803 to Falkirk) are detectable from the air. Two regiments are known
to have served at Mumrills: the *Ala Tungrorum*, a cavalry unit from
the Lower Rhineland, and the Second Cohort of Thracians, originally
recruited in Bulgaria.

West of Mumrills the course of the Wall is concealed below
housing in the old village of Laurieston, before crossing the A803 to
enter the parkland of the former **Callendar Estate***. Here the ditch
is well preserved, and can be followed over a distance of about 1 km.
(To locate the E end of the visible remains, turn left off the A803 at
a signpost for the Callendar Business Park; almost immediately the
ditch crosses the modern road at right angles. As the visitor walks W
along the crest of the ridge overlooking the lowlying Carse of Falkirk,
the ditch becomes increasingly impressive. Alternatively, the W end
of the estate can be reached by turning left off the A803 at another
roundabout, signposted to Callendar House; go left again into Seaton

Place and park at the end of the road beside Symon Tower; walk N until the ditch-hollow comes into view.) Here the ditch is still a formidable obstacle, some 18 m (60 feet) across, and the accompanying rampart survives as a low mound (FC information board).

West of Callendar Park the Wall is lost below high-rise flats before descending to the course of the now canalised East Burn. At **Kemper Avenue** beside the Burn a routine investigation in 1980, in search of the Wall before the construction of a car park, revealed an oblong building equipped with underfloor central heating, possibly a bathhouse. The car park was subsequently shortened to leave the site of the Roman building undamaged, and the course of the rampart has been indicated by careful landscaping; some of the dressed kerbstones may be visible. (Reached from the A903 by turning left at a roundabout into Arnot Street, then into Kemper Avenue; the stone base lies at the far end of the car park on the left; FC information board and HS plaque.)

Thereafter the Wall climbed to high ground S of Falkirk town centre, where a fort long presumed to lie in the area known as the Pleasance was located in 1991, when excavation on the site of a scout hut in Pleasance Lane revealed ditches perhaps defending its E side; subsequent trenching in 1993 revealed the SW corner, in Hodge St. To the W of the town-centre the visitor can pick up the ditch again at **Bantaskin** where a length of 200 m survives amid a housing development. (W of the town centre, turn S off the A903 beside a former whisky bond, now a restaurant, into Glenfuir Road, then into Anson Avenue; follow the road to the top of the ridge and park in a small, half-concealed layby on the left; the ditch lies in wooded ground above. FC information board.) Continuing W the visitor should now follow Glenfuir Road (the B816) to factory premises, then right into Tamfourhill Road. Almost immediately beyond on the left there begins a fine stretch of ditch (Fig. 73), with the low mound of the rampart visible on its S side, at **Watling Lodge****. Here the N face of the ditch had been substantially made up in antiquity to increase the efficacy of the obstacle which is still 12 m across and 5 m deep (HS plaques and FC information board). Just behind the villa of Watling Lodge (part of which stands silhouetted in the ditch at the W end of the visible stretch) was a mile-fortlet excavated in 1972–74 prior to housing development. A road led N from the fortlet to the fort at Camelon.

Beyond Watling Lodge the newly cleared ditch descends

impressively to cross low and rather marshy ground to reach again the B816, after which it enters **Tentfield Plantation***, where it can be followed without serious interruption for 2 km as far as the next fort at Rough Castle. The remains of both ditch and rampart are particularly impressive here, in the peaceful wooded setting of the plantation, especially in winter when the trees have shed their leaves and the bracken in the ditch is depressed (FC information board). Soon after entering the woodland, the ditch is crossed by a metal footbridge, in the garden of a house called Tayavalla ('the house on the Wall'). A signal-platform or 'expansion' (known as **Tentfield East**) can be seen as a mound some 10 m square attached to the rear of the rampart (opposite the entrance to Rowan Crescent). A little further W the visitor enjoys, from the upcast mound, a stunning view of the Falkirk Wheel, a newly-built award-winning mechanism for transferring canal-traffic from the higher Union Canal to the lower Forth and Clyde Canal. (This point can also be reached by a narrow track going N from the B816, just before a narrow bridge across the railway, immediately after the Canal turn. The track leads to the rampart, ditch and upcast, immediately opposite the wheel). The walker can now continue W, either following the upcast mound or the rampart itself, until the line of the frontier is cut by a quarry access road (FC information board). Just before the Wall descends to cross the quarry road, there is another 'expansion' (**Tentfield West**), attached to the S side of the rampart-mound, but it is not easy to see in the undergrowth. To either side of the quarry road the cambered mound of the Military Way is visible to the S of the Wall, beyond the double line of electricity poles. Continue along the line of the ditch, which is much disfigured by pit-heaps. Another turn to the W leads to a long straight stretch of rampart-mound and ditch; next, a stile heralds arrival at the Guardianship area of Rough Castle. (For the car user, it is advisable to turn back at the quarry road, drive to Rough Castle along the B816 via High Bonnybridge; HS signs for Rough Castle. Turn right on Foundry Road 100 m S of the Canal. Continue across the railway, past Bonnyside House, after which rampart and ditch, preserved in rough ground on the left, come into view, to a cattle grid marking the entrance to the Guardianship area; there is car parking, and the fort lies on the plateau beyond the Rowan Tree Burn.)

The fort at **Rough Castle**** is probably the most visited military installation on the Antonine Wall: its rampart stands to a height of

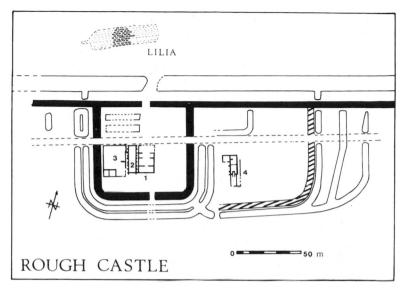

LILIA

ROUGH CASTLE

0 ▰▰▰▰ 50 m

76. Rough Castle on the Antonine Wall: ground-plan of the fort (after MacIvor, Thomas and Breeze). Note: 1 = headquarters, 2 = granary, 3 = commanding officer's house, 4 = bath-house.

1 m, and the plan of the defensive ditches is clear (HS information boards). The fort was small, scarcely more than 0.63 ha. (1.5 acres). There were four gates, one in each side, with causeways crossing the ditches to reach them (Figs. 76–77). The visitor should begin outside the N gate, and enter the fort by the causeway across the broad Antonine ditch. Straight ahead were the headquarters building and (to its right) a granary and the commanding officer's house, excavated in 1902–03, and long left exposed to public gaze; they have now been backfilled and grassed over. Turning right to the W gate of the fort, the visitor can look down over the course of the Rowan Tree Burn. On the slope are two ditches cut by a causeway. Next follow the rampart round to the S gate, and go on to the E gate, which gave access into an annexe. Just to the right (inside the annexe) was the fort bath-house. On the left (also within the annexe) is a shallow ditch turning at right angles, which may have enclosed a mile-fortlet, later replaced by the visible fort. The annexe is defended on the E by three separate ramparts and ditches, possibly testifying to successive reductions in its size. Elements of a field-system have been plotted

77. **Rough Castle on the Antonine Wall:** aerial view from the NE. Note the
course of the ditch running from bottom left to top right in the photograph
(Photo: RCAHMS, Crown copyright).

to the SE. Part of the Sixth Cohort of Nervians, originally raised
from a Belgic tribe which offered stout resistance to Caesar, formed
the garrison for a time, under the command of a legionary centurion
named as Flavius Betto.

Returning to the N gate, the visitor should cross the Antonine
ditch by the broad causeway and walk a little to the NW till a group of
oblong pits comes into view. These are the remnants of a substantial
system comprising ten rows of about 20 pits, set diagonally; the pits,
once 0.9 m deep, probably held upright sharpened stakes, concealed
from general view by brushwood. They must have been a considerable
obstacle to the unsuspecting attacker, who would fall into them
without warning, to be impaled on the stakes. Pits of this type are
described by Caesar – whose soldiers called them *lilia* ('lilies'), from a
resemblance to that flower with its vertical stem and enclosing leaves.
The visible 'lilies' at Rough Castle can still claim victims among the

unwary today. Similar pits have been identified at several points along the line of the Antonine Wall, on the flat berm between the rampart and ditch (above, p. 130).

West of Rough Castle fort, the profile of the Antonine ditch and rampart stands clear against the skyline, across the Rowan Tree Burn. The rampart survives here to a height of 1.6 m or more, the highest anywhere along the Wall. An 'expansion' (**Bonnyside East**) can just be made out attached to the S side of the rampart, some 50 m west of the entrance to the Guardianship area. It was excavated in 1957 and proved to measure about 5.3 m square, constructed of turf on a stone base. A further 'expansion' (**Bonnyside West**), this time better preserved, lies within the private grounds of Bonnyside House, just beyond the stone dyke, at a point where the Wall and ditch make a turn to the SW towards the modern village of Bonnybridge. The ditch-hollow, often filled with water or reeds, can easily be followed into the distance. It was near this spot that the legendary Scottish chieftain, Graham, broke through the Antonine Wall which in local tradition was for long to bear his name as Grahamsdyke. In truth, however, the name 'Grahamsdyke' (which survives today as a street-name at several points along the Wall) is 'grymisdyke', i.e. the strong wall. Graham and his exploits have no foundation in history. North of the modern 'Antonine Primary School' is Seabegs Motte, constructed in medieval times on the upcast of the Antonine Ditch, which served as part of its defences.

For a while the Wall is lost in modern Bonnybridge, before emerging in front of Seabegs Place farmhouse (just S of the B816), beyond which a fine stretch of the frontier can be seen in **Seabegs Wood***: ditch, upcast, rampart mound and (some 50 m to the S) the Military Way are all present (HS plaques and FC information board); excavation of the Military Way in 1962 showed that the road was *c*.7 m wide (Fig. 78). On a little plateau just beyond the W edge of the wood, on the lands of Dalnair, excavation in 1977 revealed the outlines of a mile-fortlet. A fort could be expected at Seabegs on grounds of spacing, but attempts to locate it have proved unsuccessful.

The Wall now continues W towards the village of Allandale. A short length of ditch survives N of the B816 just E of a restaurant car park. In Allandale itself the ditch can just be seen as a hollow on the N side of the road, W of a bowling green. Before the junction of the B816 with the A80 trunk road, the outline of the ditch-hollow is visible against the E boundary wall of the former Castlecary Primary School,

78. **Seabegs Wood on the Antonine Wall**: the frontier works looking W (Photo: L. Keppie).

now a private house. A fort, of 1.55 ha. (3.8 acres) with an annexe to the E, occupied the plateau at **Castlecary** overlooking the Red Burn, with a fine view N through the Denny Gap. (Turn left off the B816 just after the school, then left again to a cottage. The fort lies in the field opposite the front of the School; HS and FC information boards). Castlecary fort is mentioned by antiquaries from the mid-seventeenth century onwards, and was comprehensively dug in 1902; the fort was defended by a wall of stone, and the central buildings were stone-built. Little was learned about barracks or stores. Inscriptions found over the years testify to the presence of a First Cohort of Vardullians (from N Spain) and a First Cohort of Tungrians (from Belgium), as well as groups of legionaries. The site had already been much disturbed in 1841 by the building of the Edinburgh to Glasgow railway line which bisects the site. Nowadays little can be seen, though some stonework of the fort-wall on the E used to be visible in the field where there is a distinct ridge, and a clump of trees marks the location of the headquarters building and a granary, left exposed in 1902. A short length of the fort's N wall may be seen in a depression against the N boundary wall of the field; but the stonework is very overgrown. Stonework from Castlecary fort was transported as building material to the nearby Castle Cary, a fifteenth-century tower-house. In the garden wall of the Castle was a building stone ornamented with a horizontal phallic symbol; but it seems now to have disappeared. West of Castlecary, the Wall descends to the Red Burn, then climbs to high ground now occupied by factory premises. (Continue on the B816 across the A80.) At Garnhall beyond the railway, the ditch becomes visible again, and rapidly becomes very impressive. (Reached from a minor road beside the Castlecary Hotel; pass through a field gate on the left, beyond the car park; HS signpost and information boards). In 1994 excavation of one of two construction-camps hereabouts (named Garnhall 1 and 2) showed that its W defences did not, as hitherto supposed, underlie the Antonine Wall's E–W frontier line, but stopped just short of it, indicating their relative chronology. A ring-ditch just S of the Wall here may relate to it, but the function and dating of the site remain uncertain.

Passing in front of the site of the long-demolished farmstead of Garnhall, where some of the edging stones of the ditch may be discerned through the grass, the frontier line continues (beyond a minor road) into the former lands of **Tollpark** where it runs just N of industrial premises and later Cumbernauld Airport. Some 350 m W of the minor road, a short stretch of stone base, exposed by water action over the centuries, can be made out; it is *c*.4.5 m wide and incorporates a culvert. The ditch continues as a formidable barrier, with the upcast mound topped by a line of trees, a useful guide at a distance to its alignment. Beyond Tollpark, the Wall descends to the site of **Westerwood** fort, now an island in a sea of fairways of a golf course. (The fort can also be approached on foot from a minor road leading N from the B816 at a roundabout opposite the Old Inns filling station.) Westerwood fort, excavated in 1932, was small, scarcely more than 0.97 ha. (2.4 acres). The farm buildings occupy the fort's NE corner. The rampart, a double ditch (visible now as a single hollow), and upcast beyond are visible along the S flank of the fort, and especially at its SE corner. Farm outbuildings constructed on top of the E defences are held together against subsidence by iron clamps. An altar to the *Silvanae*, goddesses of the woodland, was found W of the fort in 1963 (now at Kinneil Museum; below, p. 189). Excavation to the S in 1974–75 failed to detect traces of civil settlement; further work in 1987–88 in advance of the laying out of the golf course revealed only scattered postholes and drainage gullies beyond the W gate. On high ground at Carrickstone, 1.5 km to the

S and best reached from Cumbernauld village, a Roman altar (the Carrick Stone) stands close to a concrete water-tower; it is increasingly threatened by housing development. No part of an inscription is now visible, and how the altar came to be at Carrickstone, if that was indeed its original location, remains unknown. Beyond Westerwood, the Wall continues through open country towards Dullatur. Just E of **East Dullatur House*** (by car best reached from Dullatur village; HS information boards), a fine stretch of ditch can be seen, some 12 m across and 3.5 m deep.

West of the Dullatur–Kilsyth road on the lands of Wester Dullatur farm the ditch shows merely as a dip along the modern field boundary, but the dip gradually broadens and deepens until it reaches **Croy Hill**** where, beyond an embankment which once supported a mineral railway, it assumes its full dimensions and can be followed uphill to Croy fort. (Best approached along a farm track off the Dullatur–Kilsyth Road about halfway between Wester Dullatur farm and the canal bridge at Craigmarloch; HS information board.) The particular reason for the splendid state of preservation hereabouts is that the ditch was cut out of solid rock – the hard dolerite of which the hill itself is largely composed. The spoil from the ditch, thrown out on the N side to form an upcast mound, remains almost as the Romans left it, its rocky make-up having resisted centuries of land improvement; meanwhile, the rampart (of turf on a stone base) has left few visible traces. We can easily imagine the consternation of the Roman work-squad detailed to dig the ditch over Croy Hill on finding rock beneath their feet instead of the usual clay or sand!

No written description is required for the visitor climbing the slope towards the summit. On the E shoulder of the Hill is the site of a fort, its position is indicated by a small group of trees. Low stone-built walls visible hereabouts are not remnants of Roman buildings but of an eighteenth-century farmhouse. Limited trenching on the fort-site in 1920, 1931 and 1935 established its outlines (about 0.78 ha./1.92 acres overall) and located some internal buildings. Several inscribed stones, now in the Museum of Scotland, Edinburgh, indicate the presence of a detachment from the Sixth Legion *Victrix*. In 1975–78 areas W, S and E of the fort were investigated in advance of the quarrying which perpetually threatens to alter the land contours hereabouts beyond recognition (Fig. 33). Some evidence of cultivation and occupation was found, together with impressive small finds including a bronze arm-purse (see Fig. 34) and part of a terracotta face-mask. Some 25 m

79. **Sculptured relief showing three legionaries,** from Croy Hill on the Antonine Wall (Photo: National Museums of Scotland).

E of the fort, a short stretch of the ditch remained undug, perhaps the result of a change-over in work-squads hereabouts.

To the W of the fort the ditch can be followed as an irregular cut on the N flank of Croy Hill which is so steep hereabouts that formal defence seems hardly necessary. Some 75 m W of Croy fort was a mile-fortlet, sited on a flat-topped hillock, first noted and tested by excavation in 1977–78. Further W, as the ground drops away and **Croy Village**** comes into view, two 'expansions' can be seen, attached to the rear of the Wall some 140 m apart. They survive impressively to a height of *c*.1.5 m.

The ditch can be followed down to the village, where a colourful new information panel, erected by the Antonine Walkway Trust, stands close to the Croy Tavern. The ditch continues W across the modern B802 in line with a track which leads W off that road towards Bar Hill (HS signpost). After 800 m the track peters out in open ground. A vacant strip in the forestry plantation marks the line of the Military Way heading uphill towards Bar Hill. The visitor should turn right to reach higher ground where the ditch soon comes into view (HS information board). From this point the visitor on foot enjoys a long vista westwards, as the ditch stretches into the distance, much as it may have looked in Roman times. After several sharp descents – the ground can be very slippery here – the ditch rises to skirt the north flank of **Castle Hill** where it overlies part of the outer defences of a small Iron Age hillfort (HS information board). At one point on the hillside the ditch seems not to have been fully dug out, perhaps because of the rock beneath. A climb to the top of Castle Hill, the summit topped by an OS triangulation cone, is well worthwhile, for it provides a view not only back to Croy, Westerwood and Castlecary, but also W to the now adjacent Bar Hill fort, and beyond it along the S flank of the Kelvin valley to Bearsden and even beyond. The watery stripe of the Forth and Clyde Canal follows the Wall's alignment westwards into the distance, with the slopes of the Campsie Hills rising on the N side of the valley. The Roman fort of Castlehill (W of Bearsden) – not to be confused with the locality currently being described – with its summit crowned by a distinctive circle of beech trees, is in view on a clear day, fully 18 km to the W, forming a convenient guide to the alignment of the frontier. Descending from Castle Hill by a winding path, the visitor arrives directly at the E gate of Bar Hill fort, while the Antonine Ditch has veered away to the right before passing along the N side of the fort towards Twechar village.

Bar Hill** fort, which the visitor on foot now approaches, is among the best-known fort-sites on the line of the Antonine Wall (Fig. 80). First noticed by antiquaries in the seventeenth century, it was comprehensively excavated in 1902–1905. The fort covered an area of about 1.4 ha. (3.4 acres), with a rampart of turf on a stone base, defended by two ditches except on the N side where there was a single ditch. The fort was not set directly, like all but one of those we have met with, against the Wall itself – the latter passed by about halfway down the N flank of Bar Hill while the fort sits squarely on its summit. The visitor entering by the E gate crosses the double ditch on a causeway which marks the line of the Military Way and should walk directly forward to the true summit of the Hill. Here facing on to the *via principalis* is the stone headquarters building, laid out for public view after re-excavation in 1979–82. There is an HS information board from which the main features and structures can be conveniently viewed. (By car it is simplest to reach Bar Hill from the W, via the B8023, turning S into Twechar village; HS signpost. Park at or opposite the war memorial in Twechar village, and walk uphill past Bar farmhouse to the top of the hill. Shortly before the large saucer-shaped water tank, turn left along a field boundary to

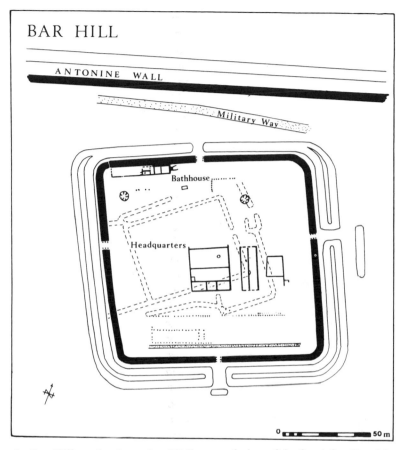

BAR HILL

ANTONINE WALL

Military Way

Bathhouse

Headquarters

0 ⸻ 50 m

80. **Bar Hill on the Antonine Wall:** ground-plan of the fort (after Keppie). Dotted lines represent the outlines of an underlying 'ditched enclosure' of uncertain date and function.

reach the fort-site with its now scanty covering of trees. In this case the visitor will arrive at the fort's SW corner; he should go directly to the summit of the hill, to the information board.)

The plan of the headquarters building is easily comprehended: the largest compartment was the front courtyard, with a stone-lined well in its E half. Behind was a covered assembly hall, and at the back a set of three rooms, of which the central compartment constituted the regimental chapel. From the 13 m-deep well came numerous

81. **Leather shoes**, from Bar Hill on the Antonine Wall. Shoes for men, women and children can be distinguished (Photo: Hunterian Museum).

stone column shafts and capitals, the wooden well-bucket, pulley wheel and winding gear, ironwork and coins (now on display in the Hunterian Museum). The S rampart of the fort followed the line of the modern field boundary. More can be seen of the W rampart and ditches, and the visitor should proceed along the *via principalis* to the W gateway, marked by a gap in the rampart. Turning then to the right, he can follow the rampart (and accompanying ditch-hollow) N to the NW corner of the fort, just inside which lay a small bath-house (HS information board). At its W end were latrines, and further E was a small hypocausted room heated by a small furnace. This was the 'hot dry' room. Further E were three heated rooms, and beyond them was a furnace; a surviving capstone from its main flue has been placed at ground level to suggest its original position. Walking E from the bath-house, the visitor quickly reaches the site of the N gate (faintly visible as a dip in the rampart mound), with a causeway across the single N ditch. At the fort's NE corner, a visible stone-lined culvert carried water through the rampart from the fort on the hilltop above. Inscriptions show that Bar Hill was garrisoned by the First Cohort of Hamians, a specialist archer unit from Roman Syria, and later

82. **Wooden wagon-wheel,** made of ash, willow and elm, with a one-piece iron tyre, from Bar Hill (Photo: Hunterian Museum).

by the First Cohort of Baetasians from the Rhineland. A broken altar recording Tanicius Verus, commanding officer of a regiment of auxiliaries, first reported built into Kilsyth Castle, may easily have derived from Bar Hill. Lost to view when the Castle was blown up by Cromwellian forces in 1650, part of it was rediscovered there in 1976.

Leaving Bar Hill by the modern gate at the SW corner of the fort, the visitor descends by the farm track to Bar farm, before which the Antonine Ditch, having passed by the fort, draws near again, and its hollow is easily made out on the right of the track. Beyond Twechar village, the Wall swings to the left past the farmhouse of Shirva (where several graveslabs and other commemorative stones were dug up in 1726–31 from the wreckage of what may have been a souterrain). Gradually the faint depression of the ditch can again be detected N of the B8023 as it approaches the farmhouse which sits within the NW quarter of **Auchendavy,** a fort of some 1.4 ha. (3.45 acres). The modern road runs through the fort on the line of its *via principalis.* The steading S of the road has recently been replaced by housing, faced with sandstone blocks deriving from demolished farm outbuildings on the site. The fort's defences are still visible on the ground, especially on the E side where there is a distinct ditch-hollow, and on the N front, where a possible causeway is faintly visible across the Antonine Ditch. Aerial photographs show that the fort was defended by three ditches. Sculptured stones, built into the farmhouse and its former adjuncts, were noted by antiquaries, but all have disappeared from view. Five altars, found in a pit S of the fort in 1771 while the Forth and Clyde Canal was being dug, were erected by Marcus Cocceius Firmus, a centurion of the Second Augustan Legion, perhaps a one-time commanding officer at the fort. These altars, and the sculptures from Shirva, are in the Hunterian Museum. Excavation in 1999, some way N of the Wall, revealed ditches and some Roman pottery.

West of Auchendavy fort, the ditch is soon lost below the embankment of the Canal. The visitor would do well now to go straight to Kirkintilloch (via the High Street, Cowgate and Union Street), to Peel Park in the centre of the town, which marks the site of the next fort on the Wall. Its precise outlines are not reliably known, but limited excavation in the park in the 1950s established the alignment of the Wall (a small but disappointing stretch of stone base, with the sad remnants of a culvert, long on view behind high railings at the NW corner of the Park, has mercifully been infilled), and confirmed that the fort lay on the rearward slope of the hill, with a splendid view across the Kelvin to the Campsie Hills. The older antiquaries assumed without question that the medieval peel (a motte now laid out as a feature within the park at its NE corner) was the Roman fort of old; in fact the peel straddles the Roman Wall and part of the fort, whose S ditches have been located at several points. Newly erected information panels highlight the history of the zone, together with markers at ground level in the shape of a locally found distance slab.

West of the fort-site in Peel Park the Wall disappears again in modern Kirkintilloch, until it emerges into open farmland at Adamslie. Little can be made out before Glasgow Bridge, where the modern A803 crosses the canal. Just E of the bridge, on higher ground above some cottages, was a mile-fortlet, seen from the air in 1951. The Wall turns slightly N to pass below the modern road, and soon the hollow of the ditch can be made out on the right as the modern road reaches the Hungryside roundabout. (Here the motorist should turn left on the A803, and may return to the line of the Wall 1 km further on via a minor road on the right, leading eventually to Cawder Church.)

The Wall continues W from the roundabout in a straight line just clear of factory premises till it reaches the site of Cadder fort where the Forth and Clyde Canal, which has again come close up against the Wall, turns sharply to the S just beyond the line of the fort's defences. The fort itself, of 1.36 ha. (3.35 acres) was entirely lost through gravel extraction in the 1930s and early 1940s. However, excavation in 1929–31 established its outlines, and revealed the layout of the internal buildings. Beyond the canal the Wall passes into the private grounds of Cawder Golf Club, formerly Cawder House, the family home of the Stirlings of Keir. Built into the wall of a ground-floor locker room inside the House is a small inscribed slab, recording building work by men of the Second Legion *Augusta*, which has been at Cawder since 1572. Vestiges of the ditch are hard to detect across the golf course before the Wall emerges on to higher ground at Wilderness Plantation. (To reach this point the motorist needs to retrace his steps from Cawder Church to the A803, then follow it towards Glasgow for 1.5 km before turning right at 'Eagle Lodge'. About 1 km after a Sports Centre, the road turns sharply left; here it rejoins the line of the Wall.) A long stretch of the Wall's course running W from this point was lost by quarrying, though the ground has since been restored. Just N of a zigzag in the modern road a mile-fortlet was revealed from the air in 1951 at Wilderness Plantation, and excavated in advance of expected quarrying in 1965–66. (The quarrying never took place.) The ditch can be followed W from this point, as a hollow in open farmland N of the road, and where it is crossed by the modern road a short, deeper stretch is filled with water, a good indicator of its position. Aerial reconnaissance has hereabouts revealed three so-called 'ditched enclosures' attached to the rampart; one (at Buchley farm) was excavated in 1980, without clarifying its function. From Wilderness Plantation onwards the modern road overlies the Roman ditch, before the latter veers away N, as the ground drops away, to descend to the site of Balmuildy fort on a low plateau overlooking the River Kelvin, with fine views up the valley of the Blane Water. Balmuildy was excavated in 1912–14 and much of its layout established, including a stone headquarters building, commanding officer's house and granaries set within a stone rampart-wall, as well as two bath-houses, one inside the fort, and the other (more elaborate) within an annexe E of the fort. The fort itself, with an area of 1.7 ha. (4.1 acres), was built before the Wall itself, with projecting 'wing-walls' designed to join up with the Wall when its builders reached Balmuildy. Nothing can be made out on the ground today.

Next the Wall turns sharply N to cross the Kelvin. Large dressed sandstone blocks, parts of the piers of a bridge crossing the river here, were dredged up in 1941 and in 1982; the blocks were conspicuous by the cramp-holes recessed into their sides to hold them fast together against the surge of the river.

Beyond the river the Wall heads due N (beside the A879) to the heights of Summerston, where the ditch can be observed turning sharply to the W behind some cottages. After crossing the A879 it ascends to the summit of Crow Hill; on the E slope of the hill a mile-fortlet was identified in 1980. An 'Antonine Wall feature' has been incorporated into the nearby Dobbies Garden Centre at Temple of Boclair south of the B8049. Westwards from the summit of the Hill the ditch-line can be followed along field boundaries until it crosses the B8049. On the W side of the road embankment here, the hollow of the ditch is visible as it crosses a small field before entering Douglas Park Golf Course. Following the natural crest of the ground it next reaches **Hillfoot Cemetery***. Here two fine stretches of the stone base can be seen, exposed during landscaping of the cemetery early in the twentieth century. The visitor entering the cemetery should veer to the right to reach its E boundary-wall on the crest of the hill, where close to and all but protruding from the modern ground surface is the stone base of the Antonine Wall, 4.3 m wide with finely dressed kerbs and a rubble core incorporating a drainage culvert. The second stretch of visible base lies further down the hillside, nearer the cemetery entrance. Because the Wall has turned sharply S following ground contours, the second stretch appears to visitors (and indeed is) at right angles to the first, the cause of some confusion! The base here, where it descends a sharp slope, was built originally to the standard width of 4.3 m, but was subsequently broadened to 5 m and a second layer of stones was laid down on the upper part of the slope, perhaps to improve stability of the overlying turfwork after a collapse. This stretch too incorporates a culvert (Fig. 72).

Soon after, the Wall turns again to the W (a faint curving hollow in the cemetery marks the line of the ditch), and can be followed across the boundary fence into rough ground beyond. Here both ditch and rampart-mound can be observed along the N ends of gardens of **Boclair Road**, except where shielded from view by impenetrable hedges, until they are finally lost among trees and shrubbery.

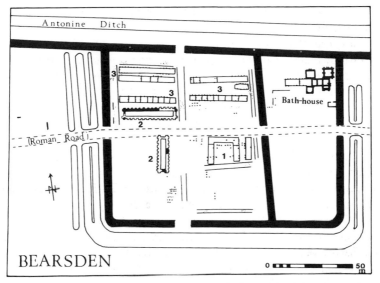

83. **Bearsden on the Antonine Wall**: ground-plan of the fort (after Breeze). Note: 1 = workshop(?), 2 = granaries, 3 = barracks and stores.

Returning to the cemetery, the visitor should now proceed by way of Boclair Road, across the road junction with the A81 at the bottom of the hill, into Roman Road, so named in the nineteenth century because it follows the line of the Military Way. The Wall itself ran along the S lip of a defile containing the Manse Burn.

Soon the modern road rises to a plateau which marked the site of the next fort, **Bearsden****, passing through the site on the line of the fort's *via principalis*; the fort thus lies both N and S of the modern road (Fig. 83). In the late 1970s the entire N half of the fort and its annexe was redeveloped, with four large sandstone mansions of the Victorian age replaced by numerous maisonettes. Excavation from 1973 onwards in advance of the housebuilding produced a fairly complete plan of the N half of the fort, which had an area of about 1.2 ha. (2.9 acres) overall, with barracks and storebuildings, and a large stone-built granary (Fig. 41), all of which lay scarcely 30 cm below the lawns and shrubberies of the Victorian villas and had amazingly survived landscaping and terracing in the 1880s. The Antonine Wall itself, on the crest of the slope overlooking the Manse Burn, had been swept away, but the accompanying ditch was located, as were the E and W

84. **Excavation in progress at Bearsden bath-house**, 1979 (Photo: L. Keppie).

ramparts of the fort, and ditches beyond them. In an annexe lying to the E was the bath-house, the discovery of which was the highlight of the excavations (Fig. 84), and which has now been laid out as an ancient monument, though tightly hedged about by the modern development. (On Roman Road, 300 m E of Bearsden Cross; HS signposts.) An information board provides a valuable and colourful guide to the layout of rooms. A timber-framed changing room led to a cold room and then to a sequence of heated compartments; opening separately off the cold room was a hot dry room, of which the floor is well preserved with a channelled hypocaust below and the furnace mouth beyond (Fig. 20). Opposite was a semicircular cold-plunge bath. A fine sandstone head of a goddess, sometimes identified as *Fortuna* (Good Fortune), found in the plunge-bath in 1973, is now in the Hunterian Museum (Fig. 85). In the furthest heated room (the hot room), and in the hot dry room, heat was directed up the walls not in the usual clay piping but behind thin stone slabbing kept clear of the walls by stone 'headers'. Just to the N are the walls of a room supported by buttresses. This was evidently intended as a heated compartment, but it seems not to have come into use. Nearby

85. **Head of a goddess,** perhaps *Fortuna* (Good Fortune), from Bearsden; about half life-size (Photo: Hunterian Museum).

to the SE is a small rectangular structure, identifiable as a latrine block. Analysis of sewage deposits in a nearby annexe ditch brought the revelation that the soldiers' diet was primarily vegetarian, and had included raspberries, strawberries and figs, along with opium poppy and coriander seeds for flavouring bread.

South of Roman Road, within the grounds of 'Maxholme', now a Baptist Church, limited excavation in flowerbeds and under lawns and driveways revealed a second stone granary, and traces of other buildings including a workshop. The sharp fall-away in the ground S of 'Maxholme' marks the S limit of the fort, with a broad ditch beyond. An inscribed building stone found near the stone-built granary N of Roman Road indicates that some part of the work was carried out by men of the Twentieth Legion.

To the W of Bearsden fort, the Wall continues due W across the A809 into gardens on the N side of Thorn Road (where a short stretch of stone base discovered in 1973 has been laid out as a garden feature).

Thereafter the Wall turned to the NW (some stonework can be seen in gardens in Colquhoun Drive and Milverton Avenue). A further turn to the W brought the frontier to a ridge where the course of the rampart and ditch is preserved in an area of grassland known as Roman Park (reached from **Westbourne Crescent**, shortly before its junction with Ballaig Avenue; look for a narrow path leading uphill opposite the house 'Wayside'. Alternatively this stretch is accessible from the W, via Iain Road, by steps between nos. 85 and 87). The course of the Wall is defined on the ground by concrete markers. At the W end of the stretch an area of stone-base cleared in 1963 lies exposed but very overgrown behind railings; a matching ditch-section was backfilled in the 1970s. Further W the line of the Wall was left clear during housing developments in the 1960s (between Rosslyn Road and Antonine Road; HS plaques).

The Wall now climbs to the heights of **Castlehill**, surmounted by a circle of beech trees. (Just S of the A810, beyond the W outskirts of Bearsden. Turn left off the A810, immediately after Antonine Road, to park at a small telephone exchange, and walk uphill. The hedge-line straight ahead marks the course of the Antonine Wall running W towards the hill itself.) Older antiquaries believed that the fort lay entirely within the tree-circle, but aerial photography has shown that it lay partly on sloping ground to the E. No excavation has taken place on the hilltop, but when trees are blown over in a winter's gale pottery fragments have been found in their roots. A small raised plateau at the NW corner of the hill, within the tree-circle, may mark the site of a mile-fortlet preceding the fort, and subsequently linked to its W defences (compare Duntocher, below, p. 155). Of the fort itself (1.41 ha./3.5 acres) there is very little to see: a slight depression running S a little to the E of the raised plateau may mark the position of the W defences of the fort; the S defences lie a little beyond the field boundary on the S side of the hilltop. The garrison of the fort was at one time the Fourth Cohort of Gauls; an altar dedicated by its prefect and honouring the 'Goddesses of the Paradeground' (a favourite object of military veneration) was found there in 1826. Part of what seems likely to have been a Roman sculptured slab was recently identified built into a circular outbuilding at nearby Castlehill farm. From the summit of the hill the visitor can on a clear day see most of the Wall forts E to Bar Hill, and to the W the fort-site at Duntocher (though not Old Kilpatrick) is in view, along with those at Bishopton and Barochan on the far bank of the Clyde (above p. 105).

From Castlehill the Wall descends to the SW along a hedge-line, crossing Peel Glen Road to reach the Peel Burn. Beyond the burn the Wall rises to cross Hutcheson Hill, its ditch scarcely visible except when low winter sunlight accentuates the hollow; then it descends to the Cleddans Burn on the N outskirts of Drumchapel, with the ditch-hollow clearly visible flanked by thick gorse bushes. Just E of the burn a magnificent distance slab (Figs. 28–29) was ploughed up in 1969. Beyond the Burn the ditch becomes visible again, as a dip close to the edge of a field, on the S side of a track leading to Cleddans farmhouse. On high ground beyond the farm – the only point in the 3 km stretch between Castlehill and Duntocher where both these fort-sites are simultaneously in view – a mile-fortlet was found by trial excavation in 1980. The Wall's course beyond Cleddans is overlaid by the modern farmtrack until it is lost in the edge of the much expanded village of **Duntocher**. Nothing can be seen until the Wall climbs to the summit of Golden Hill, which was the site of a small fort excavated in 1947–51 before the S half of the hilltop was built over by housing (Fig. 86). The rest lies within a park. (From the A82 at a roundabout take the A8014 towards Duntocher; as it veers right at a 'funeral home', turn

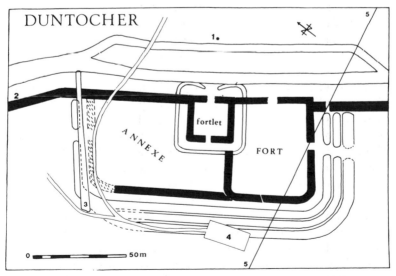

86. **Duntocher on the Antonine Wall:** ground-plan of the fortlet and fort (after Robertson). Note: 1 = flagpole, 2 = visible stretch of stone rampart-base, 3 = hedge, 4 = former swings, 5 = boundary fence of housing development.

left on to Milton Douglas Road and follow its continuation, Roman Road; watch for the Antonine Sports Centre, and park opposite it at a church. A little beyond is a war memorial, from which a path leads up to the hilltop.) A short length of the Wall's stone base, left open after excavation in 1947, is displayed behind railings. It is sometimes very overgrown, and the culvert which crosses the base at a slant is hardly visible now. This stretch of base provides a useful indicator of the Wall's alignment. Just to the S of its line, immediately behind the war memorial, part of the fort bath-house, originally discovered and excavated in 1775–78, was located again in 1978. A broad shallow hollow representing the ditch can be followed uphill to the summit; but on the hilltop there is nothing for today's visitor to see, apart from a fine view W towards the River Clyde. The earliest structure on the summit was a mile-fortlet, constructed in advance of the Wall itself. Initially examined in 1947–51, the fortlet's rampart was completely exposed in 1977–78, in the hope that it might become a permanent 'ancient monument'; but the trenches were backfilled. The fort itself (of 0.26 ha./0.64 acres) was built to the E of the fortlet, incorporating the latter's E rampart in its defences. A 'Roman garden' was laid out in 1978 on lower ground, N of the fort, with appropriate plants and shrubbery; but there is nothing to inform the present-day visitor of its significance.

Beyond Duntocher Burn – a slab on the bridge, erected in 1772 by Lord Blantyre, is often mistakenly identified as Roman because of its Latin inscription – the Wall, now increasingly overlooked by the Kilpatrick Hills, is lost again in the village of Duntocher, though the V-shape of the ditch could once be espied in the corrugated iron sheeting bounding a football pitch. Thereafter the Wall follows the line of Beeches Road, and then a grassy track, to pass in front of Carleith farm. West of Carleith it continues to follow a modern track towards a clump of trees; thereafter it is completely lost in farmland before rising to the farmhouse of Mount Pleasant. The hollow of the ditch was visible in the farmyard until destroyed by wartime bombing in 1941. Beyond Mount Pleasant the Wall descends to its terminus at Old Kilpatrick, its course cut by the A82 'boulevard' and then by housing. The fort site at Old Kilpatrick was excavated in 1923–24 prior to house-building. (Reached from the A82 by turning left, immediately after the access route to the Erskine Bridge, and then right on to the A814; stop in the village at a now disused bus garage on the left; this overlies the W half of the fort.) Future redevelopment

87. **Altar to Jupiter,** from Old Kilpatrick on the Antonine Wall, found in 1969. It was erected by the First Cohort of Baetasians under its prefect Publicius Maternus (Photo: Hunterian Museum).

of the bus garage may allow, at the very least, an opportunity for the fort-site to be marked out or otherwise commemorated. Old Kilpatrick fort was quite large (1.91 ha./4.7 acres), and evidently built before the Wall builders arrived. The headquarters and a granary were in stone, with timber-framed stores and barracks to front and rear. In 1969 a splendid altar dedicated to Jupiter by the fort's garrison, the First Cohort of Baetasians, was found lying in the outer ditch on the

88. **Distance slab** from Old Kilpatrick on the Antonine Wall, erected by men of the Twentieth Legion to record the completion of 4411 feet of the work (Photo: Hunterian Museum).

NE side, during the digging of an inspection pit in now-demolished garage premises N of the A814 (Fig. 87); a group of houses currently occupies the spot. The area between the fort and the River Clyde (reached by turning off the A814 into Gavinburn Place and then right into Portpatrick Road) contained the fort bath-house and other buildings, which were swept away in the building of the Forth and Clyde Canal in 1790. The splendid little canal bridge at Ferrydyke, between the fort-plateau and the river, marks the Wall's course as it approaches the Clyde. Sometime before 1684 a distance slab of the Twentieth Legion, showing a reclining figure of the goddess Victory holding a wreath to celebrate the success of the Roman army, was found at Ferrydyke cottages; it may have stood at the W terminus of the Wall (Fig. 88). Another stone, probably a distance slab, was seen in the 1750s serving as a threshold in one of the cottages, but it has long since disappeared from view. For the Wall builders this was the end of 60 km of building work.

12

SCOTLAND NORTH OF
THE ANTONINE WALL

From Forth to Tay

Just 1.5 km N of the Antonine Wall, on the banks of the River Carron
and overlooking the Forth, lay the fort at **Camelon**, on a natural land
route to the N, between the Forth and the Kilsyth Hills. The plateau
occupied by the fort is now surrounded on three sides by a golf
course, and on the fourth by a railway line and factories. (To reach
it, take the A9 NW out of Falkirk; 700 m after it diverges from the
A803, look for a golf clubhouse on the left; ask at the clubhouse for
permission to cross the course to the plateau behind, which is fringed
by hawthorn bushes; an old stone bridge crossing the railway line is a
convenient landmark, lying close to the position of the fort's S gate.
Alternatively, continue N on the A9 for a further 500 m to an access
road into the course beside a bus garage. This road heads directly
towards the plateau.) When the plateau is reached, the fort-platform
is easily discerned, with low bankings representing the rampart on
the W, N and E sides, with dips in the bank marking gateways, most
obviously on the E side. This was the site of an Antonine fort, which
had an area of 2.91 ha. (7.1 acres), with internal buildings entirely of
stone. The zone to the S, across the railway, was very probably the
site of the Flavian fort here (and later an Antonine annexe); it has
long since been built over by factories. Redevelopment work in the
1970s was preceded by excavation, adding to our appreciation of the
Flavian occupation. Further redevelopment is now in prospect. The
significance of Camelon as a staging post for forces moving N–S in
Roman Scotland has been revealed over the years with the discovery
from the air of at least ten temporary camps lying both W and S of
the fort. Long identified as a 'Pictish City' before being recognised
as a Roman fort, Camelon has attracted attention for its possible link
with Camelot and the legendary King Arthur.

Three km N of Camelon there stood until 1743 a beehive-shaped
stone structure (Fig. 90), over 6 m in diameter and some 7 m high,
known from medieval times as 'Arthur's O'on' (= Oven). Antiquarian

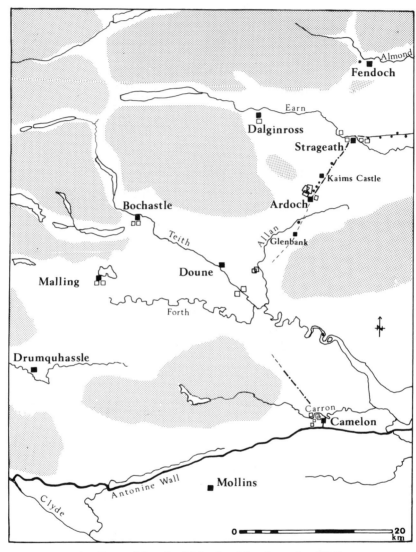

89. **Central Scotland North of the Antonine Wall.**

90. **Arthur's O'on** (reproduced from Alexander Gordon, *Itinerarium Septentrionale*, 1726)

writers reported sculptured figures on its outer facade, and in about 1700 the single finger of a bronze statue was found inside. The precise function of the O'on – a Roman date is assumed – has not been established; we could most easily think of it as a tomb, but some scholars have argued that it was a victory monument, associated with the campaigns of Agricola, Lollius Urbicus or even Severus. A full-size 'replica' of Arthur's O'on, built in 1767, surmounts the stable block of Penicuik House, the former home of the antiquary Sir John Clerk.

At nearby Dunipace aerial survey brought to light a camp of 55 ha. (130 acres) on the N bank of the Carron, 2.5 km NW of Camelon, the first in a series of such camps extending N to the South Esk or even beyond (below, p. 183); some faint traces of its ramparts can be seen at the corner-angles.

The main Roman road to the north continued from the N gate of Camelon fort towards Stirling, but is scarcely visible except in woods NW of Torwood village. The precise point where the Roman road crossed the Forth has never been established, but camps have been found beside the river W of Stirling itself, and a fort of 2.6 ha. (6.3 acres) has been identified from the air at Doune, high above the junction between the Ardoch Burn and the River Teith, so that it seems possible now that the Romans' crossing-point lay much further W than hitherto supposed. Excavation in 1999, in advance of the construction of a nursery school, exposed its defences on the NW side, bread ovens set into the back of the rampart, and timber-framed buildings, one possibly a hospital, with finds confirming a Flavian occupation.

From the Forth the road continued NE up the valley of the Allan Water, past a fortlet at Glenbank near Greenloaning (where a watch-tower guarding the road has recently been identified and examined) to Ardoch beside the River Knaik. **Ardoch**** must rank as the single most impressive Roman fort in Scotland (Fig. 91) because of the fine state of preservation of its defences. (From the A9 at Greenloaning follow the A822 to Braco village; park at the N edge of the village, at a small car park on the left (information panel highlighting the 'Braco Village Trail'), and walk across a bridge to an access point at the fort's W gate where there is a sign for the fort; alternatively there is a lay-by 150 m beyond the bridge, but beware of fast-moving traffic. An oblong panel set into the stone wall on the E side of the road between the lay-by and the bridge commemorates a visit by Queen Victoria and Prince Albert in 1842. (Group visits should be notified in advance to the Factor, Estate Office, Burnside of Balhaldie, Dunblane, 01786-824000). The rampart of the fort stands to a height of about 2 m, and the ditches have a depth of over 2 m, almost as left by the Romans 1800 years ago. (The visitor should walk round the ramparts in an anti-clockwise direction, stopping to admire the defences when he reaches the E gate. Walk out on to the causeway there to get the best view.) The multiplication of ditches (five in all) on the E and N sides is the result, it now seems, not of anxiety over the fort's security against attack, but of successive reductions in its size, as the garrison itself was cut back: the outer ditches on each side are the earliest, and the inner circuits were added later (Fig. 92). The sequence is clearest

91. **Ardoch, Perth & Kinross:** aerial view of the fort from the N, showing its ramparts and defensive ditches. (Photo: Colin Martin.)

on the N side of the fort (walk round now to the N gate), where stubs of the original rampart still stand, cut by the later ditches. The bank beyond the outer ditches is thought to be relatively modern. The W defences were destroyed by the modern road, and those on the S have been marred by cultivation. The fort, occupied in both Flavian and Antonine periods, was comprehensively excavated in 1896–97; the internal buildings seem to have been of timber in both major periods, though a single barrack in stone was found. Nothing is visible of the internal arrangements – the enclosure in the middle of the fort is a remnant of a medieval graveyard with a rectangular chapel at its centre. Initially the fort had an area of about 3.15 ha. (7.78 acres), but by the close of the Antonine period it had been reduced to about 2.3 ha. (5.7 acres).

Ardoch fort did not stand alone. To the N was an annexe, of which the ramparts can be traced on the ground. Cutting through the N part of the annexe are the defences of a large temporary camp of some 55 ha.

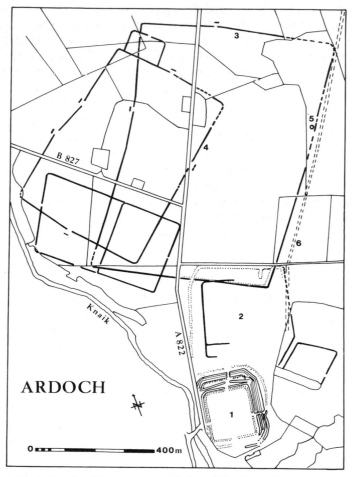

92. **Ardoch, Perth & Kinross:** ground-plan of the fort and marching camps (after St Joseph). Note: 1 = fort, 2 = annexe (within which are the ditches of a small camp), 3 = 55 ha. (130-acre) camp, 4 = 25 ha. (63-acre) camp, 5 = watch-tower in Blackhill Wood, 6 = Roman road northwards to Kaims Castle.

(130 acres), perhaps belonging to Severus' campaigns, which overlie a small double-ditched watch-tower (named Blackhill Wood) lying one Roman mile N of the fort (below, p. 165). Other camps, including one of 25 ha. (63 acres), lie some distance from the fort to the NW. Parts of these installations, surviving in the heather-covered landscape, were

initially surveyed by General Roy; gaps in our knowledge have been filled over the years through aerial photography when the outlines of the camps have appeared as cropmarks in cultivated ground. It is perhaps best for the visitor who has drunk his fill of the fort-site to pass through the ditches on its N side by a causeway, and veer left to reach the A822 at a metal field gate. Here look right to see the defensive ditch of the Annexe, which should now be followed N for 300 m into bracken-covered ground; the ditch is accompanied by a 1.5 m-high rampart bank. Just beyond the area of rough ground, the annexe ditch cuts through the S rampart of the 55 ha. camp. The annexe ditch soon turns E to run along the S side of a minor road to Auchterarder. As the annexe defences run E they become less and less impressive, and the line is obscured by modern bankings, until (just opposite a wooden gate on the far side of the modern road) the annexe ditch seems to be cut through in turn by the ditch of the 55 ha. camp.

Some further stretches of the rampart and ditch of both the 25 ha. and 55 ha. camps are to be seen in rough ground W of the A822. (Go N on the A822 to its junction with the B827 signposted for Comrie; about 50 m along the secondary road look at the sloping ground on the right to see a length of rampart of the 25 ha. camp covered by heather; HS information board). Some 200 m further on, also on the right, there begins a long stretch of some 300 m of the rampart and accompanying ditch of the 55 ha. camp, running N–S. The low banking of the rampart can be followed N across the heather-covered hillside; close to the far end is a break in the rampart, masked by a traverse. Some distance to the N can be seen a 250 m-length of mound running E–W, which overlies the N rampart of the 25 ha. camp. Most probably the visible mound is fairly modern. (This stretch can also be seen from the A822, at 50 m N of Blackhills cottage.) The Roman road going N from Ardoch was flanked by watch-towers at roughly one Roman mile intervals; four such towers are known, the nearest to Ardoch lying in Blackhill Wood (above).

At **Kaims Castle***, about halfway between Ardoch and the next fort at Strageath, lies a fortlet, almost square in shape, *c.*30 m x 30 m, within a single, almost circular ditch. (On the A822 3 km N of Ardoch and 4 km S of Muthill village, opposite the driveway to Orchill Castle; the fortlet lies in rough pasture W of the modern road, beyond Kaims Cottage. Go through a wooden farm-gate immediately S of the cottage; the fortlet lies 60 m in front on a prominent knoll.)

Kaims Castle is among the best-preserved fortlets in Scotland, with the rampart still standing to a height of over 1.5 m, and the ditch 3 m wide and 1 m deep within an upcast mound. There was a single gate, on the E side, facing the Roman road, which was reached by means of a causeway across the ditch. The interior of the fortlet, excavated in 1900, was paved with cobbles, surely in a secondary phase, but no structures were located or small finds made.

Some 6 km further N is the next fort, at **Strageath**, overlooking the River Earn. (From the A822 at Muthill where the main road turns to the left at Muthill Old Church and Tower, go right and then left at a sign 'Strageath 2'; turn right again almost immediately and follow the road for 3 km to Strageath Mains Farm. Park at the farmhouse and request access. The fort (of 1.8 ha./4.44 acres) lies on the plateau to the SE. Go uphill along a field boundary marked with trees from the front of the farm buildings, then left along another tree-lined fence. About 120 m into this second field note the low bank which represents the rampart of an annexe; some 80 m further on is the fort-platform, with the rampart surviving as a low mound; continue along the fence which turns right and then left.) The second fence-corner lies atop the N rampart of the fort, which (if the visitor looks E towards the river) can be seen turning the NE angle. Aerial photography over many years has revealed the outlines of a complex ditch-system. Excavations in 1973–86 under the auspices of the Scottish Field School of Archaeology established a detailed plan of much of the interior of the fort; small finds included a 'pig' of lead and some scale-armour. The fort was in use in both Flavian and Antonine periods. Its importance came from its position guarding the crossing of the Earn.

Beyond Strageath the Roman road continues to the NE to cross the River Earn near Innerpeffray (where there are two temporary camps), then turns E to ascend the **Gask Ridge**, an E–W spine of land N of the Earn with fine views N towards Glenalmond, as well as back into the hollow of Strathearn. A rutted road surface, perhaps Roman, was revealed in 2004, when a section was cut in a deep cutting concealed by woodland on the E side of the Earn, S of the historic Innerpeffray Library. Where it passed along the Gask Ridge the road was flanked by watch-towers at roughly 1 km intervals; a dozen are known, placed a little way to one or other side of the road. The Gask Ridge 'frontier system', sometimes defined as incorporating all known installations between the River Carron via Stirling to the Tay, is currently the subject of a detailed research project. Several towers, long known to

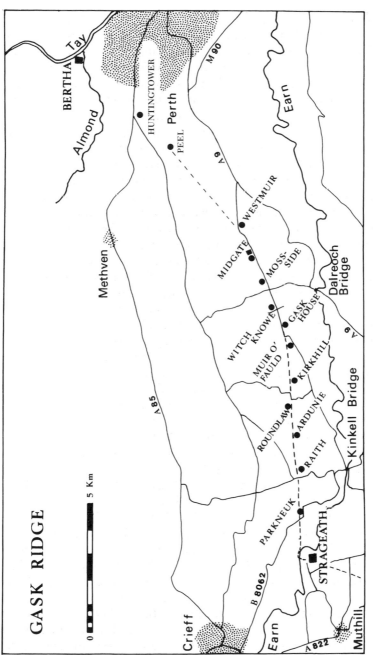

93. Gask Ridge, Perth & Kinross, showing sequence of watch-towers.

antiquaries, were excavated in 1900; others have been located more recently through aerial photography. The towers were of a standard plan: about 4 m square, with substantial timber uprights at the four corners, probably supporting a structure two or (better) three storeys high. Each tower was enclosed by a rampart and a single ditch, with a gap to allow access from the road. The spoil from the ditch was used to form a counterscarp bank. Seven of the towers are visible today, in varying degrees of impressiveness; those most worth visiting are at Parkneuk, Kirkhill and Muir O'Fauld (Fig. 93). The visitor should not underestimate the time needed to find some of the sites in dense woodland, though recent work by the Historic Scotland has made access easier at several sites. The line of the Roman road can be followed on foot from Ardunie farm to Midgate, though the view to N and S is generally obscured by forestry.

At the W end of the Gask Ridge above the Earn crossing is the watchtower at **Parkneuk** (Fig. 23). (Reached by taking the B8062 from Crieff or from Auchterarder; 2.5 km N of Kinkell Bridge, the road swings sharply to the left at some woodland; look for an access road into the wood and park there; pass through a wooden gate, and 60 m beyond, turn sharply right to see the watch-tower in rough grassland *c*.50 m beyond, increasingly overgrown by bracken.) The ground plan was established by excavation in 1968. The ditch is now 3.5 m wide and 0.75 m deep, with the counterscarp bank prominent. Little is preserved of the rampart, but there is a causeway across the ditch N to the Roman road which survives in the woodland as a low cambered mound 30 m in front. Walking back to the modern road, the visitor should stop at the wooden gate, and look forward *c*.10 m to left and right, to see a prominent bank which constitutes the N rampart of the larger of two temporary camps lying beside the Earn at Innerpeffray; the accompanying ditch is on the woodland side of the bank.

To see other towers of the Gask Ridge system, the visitor should go via Kinkell Bridge to Trinity Gask, then follow signs to Madderty; 700 m N of the Trinity Gask Church the road swings sharply E to follow the Roman highway. From this point the visitor can walk W for 1.3 km to the site of **Ardunie** tower (HS signpost at the public road and information board at the site), but the surrounding ditch is but a faint hollow. More profitably, follow the Roman road E from this point into woodland along an estate road; after 500 m, look for a path on the right (discreet HS signpost at ankle-level) across duckboards to the watch-tower of **Kirkhill***, where a circular ditch

0.5 m deep, broken by a causeway, enclosed the platform where the tower once stood (HS information board). The Roman road can be followed E on foot along the spine of the ridge to **Muir O' Fauld*** tower. (The motorist needs to return to Trinity Gask, turn left and continue for 3 km; where the road swings to the left and then almost immediately sharp right, the line of the Roman road is again reached. This point can also be accessed from the A9 at Dalreoch, signposted Findo Gask.) Park at the double bend in the road, and walk W past a locked metal gate for 350 m. An HS signpost on the left guides the visitor across duckboards to the tower, enclosed within a fence and sturdy gate (HS information board). All the constituent features are visible here: a low rampart within its surrounding ditch, broken by a causeway N to the road, and counterscarp bank beyond. When vegetation is low, the positions of the four post-pits which supported the timber tower can be seen.

Return now to the modern highway; some 500 m E of the double bend is another tower, named **Gask House**. The site lies just S of the road but can be difficult to find in dense woodland. (Where the road tops a slight rise, look for a break in the low stone dyke on the right, and head S into the wood for 20 m.) The ditch is well preserved and its outer edges are marked by single fenceposts. The next tower in the sequence, at **Witch Knowe**, is overgrown, but repays a visit. (Continue E to the lodge-cottage at the driveway to Gask House, and take the track (opposite) leading N for 150 m until wire fencing terminates on the right. Walk E into the woodland for *c*.100 m, crossing an old plantation banking, after which the ditch, here 0.5 m deep, comes into view.) The site of another tower can be viewed at **Midgate**, a further 2.5 km to the E atop a natural E–W ridge. (Opposite the unsignposted access road to Blairbell, climb on to a double hillock.) The ditch of the tower, atop the more westerly of the two hillocks, is poorly represented by a hollow 0.25 m deep, its course marked by thistles, enclosing an area *c*.12 m square overall. More obvious to the visitor is the enclosing ditch of an adjacent fortlet, on the hilltop immediately to the E; part of the site lies E of the boundary fence, in woodland. The visitor returning S to the line of the A9 at Dalreoch has a fine view over Strathearn and the distinctively craggy profile of Craig Rossie, a contender for the site of *Mons Graupius* (above, p. 8).

The precise context in which these towers were built is not certain: excavation at Gask House tower in 1965 produced a small fragment of *mortarium* rim, dated to the period *c.*AD 70–95, which has been used to date the system to the Flavian period. Scholars have seen the system of towers N of Ardoch and along the Gask Ridge as a patrolled frontier line, perhaps belonging to the time when forts N of the Earn were abandoned (c. 85–90 AD), making the Gask Ridge in effect the N limit of the Roman province. But some confirmation of the dating would be welcome before too many hypotheses are constructed.

The valley of the Earn was traversed by Roman troops from the time of Agricola onwards: camps of *c.*46.5 ha. (115 acres) at Dunning and Abernethy are dated to this time, and another member of the same series is suspected S of the Severan fortress at Carpow (below). Part of the N side of the camp-defences at **Dunning** can be seen, increasingly overgrown and hard to find, in Kincladie Wood. (0.8 km N of Dunning on Perth Road, the B934; park at the SW corner of the wood, and walk forwards *c.*80 m to the top of a small rise.) The rampart stands 0.6 m high with a ditch to its right, extending into the wood for 130 m; the modern road passes through a gateway in the camp defences. The gap was masked by a traverse *c.*15 m in front of the rampart. The traverse is still visible, when the undergrowth is low, close up against the modern fence beside the road. Discovery of Antonine pottery during excavation in 1992 may indicate later reuse. The heights of Craig Rossie are in full view. An information board at the twelfth century St Serf's Church, Dunning (which now houses the magnificent early ninth-century Dupplin Cross), relates the camp to the present-day layout of the village.

Carpow, conceivably the place named *Orrea* by the geographer Ptolemy, lies just E of the junction between the Earn and the Tay, with extensive views across the Firth. (In open farmland, north of the A913, 3 km W of Newburgh; for access to the site, ask at Carpow House.) An old tradition of Roman antiquities was confirmed in 1961–62; excavation was renewed in 1974–79 (Fig. 94). The fortress, of some 11 ha. (27.5 acres), was set within a rampart and double ditch. The gates were stone-built: two have yielded fragments of stone commemorative tablets now in Dundee Museum. The inscription on the E gate slab has been restored to show a dedication to the Emperor Caracalla, presumably in AD 211–212, shortly before the final Roman withdrawal from Scotland; sculptured motifs include emblems of the Second Legion *Augusta*, which is thus identifiable as the builder. Within the fortress, excavation revealed the headquarters building and a commanding officer's sizeable mansion; roofing tiles here bear

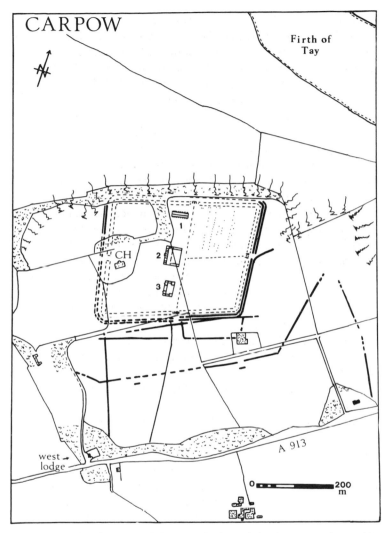

94. **Carpow, Perth & Kinross:** ground-plan of the fortress and marching camps (after St Joseph and Wilkes). Note: 1 = granary, 2 = headquarters, 3 = residence of legion's commander; CH = Carpow House.

95. **Carpow, Perth & Kinross:** aerial view of the Severan fortress from the NE. Note the broad ditches on the E and S sides, and a road issuing from the E gateway (Photo: Colin Martin).

the name of the Sixth Legion, with an added title *Britannica*, which it apparently acquired in AD 210–211. A granary in stone, or on stone foundations, was also explored, and some trial work was undertaken on one area of barracks which were of timber. Carpow fortress could have housed about 3000 men. Little can be seen today, but the ripple of the S defences can be made out in the fields E of Carpow House, and in summer drought conditions the lines of ditches on the E and S sides of the fortress are visible to the passer-by from the adjacent A913 (Fig. 95).

In the interior of Fife, a map of half a century ago would have shown no Roman sites, but three camps are now known, probably indicating that the Romans penetrated into Fife by the central E-W route with the Ochil Hills on one side and the Lomond Hills (an early candidate for *Mons Graupius*) on the other, reaching and following the River Eden, perhaps aiming for St Andrews Bay where a fort would not now be completely unexpected. One camp, at Edenwood, of 25 ha. (63 acres), could testify to a Severan taskforce operating on this route; some parts of the rampart may be detected. Doubtless, too,

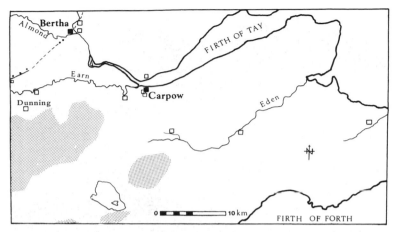

96. The Fife Peninsula.

Roman forces followed the S coast of the Fife peninsula, but no sites are known there as yet.

The Highland Line Forts

West of the Roman road from the Forth to the Tay is a group of forts established by Agricola or his immediate successor at the mouths of various Highland glens (see Fig. 89). Most scholars believe that they were intended to prevent access to Roman-held territory by the tribesmen of the mountains beyond. The best known is at **Fendoch** (see Fig. 18), close to the mouth of the Sma' [i.e. Small] Glen, where the River Almond issues from a narrow defile and descends into Strathalmond. (For the traveller from the S, the easiest approach is from Crieff, turning off the A85 on to the A822 at Gilmerton; look for the junction of the A822 with the B8063; park at the junction.) The fort itself, of 1.8 ha. (4.5 acres), lay on a levelled platform 500 m to the SE, slightly back from the entrance to the Sma' Glen, with a range of hills behind it. On the ground today a faint ridge marks the line of the ramparts, and the hollow of a ditch can be made out at the SW corner of the fort. The site was excavated by Sir Ian Richmond in 1936–38, and its ground plan is well known; the fort probably housed an 800-strong regiment of auxiliary infantry.

On high ground W of the modern road into the glen, *c.*350 m N of the junction, lies a probable watch-tower, not yet found when the excavation of the fort itself took place. (Look for the third hillock from the modern road; a narrow path leads to the summit.) The site (**Sma' Glen***) has not been excavated, and some have doubted a Roman date for the earthwork, but it enjoys a good forward view into the glen, and is within easy sight of the fort, to pass back information about hostile activity. The rampart is set within a single ditch, which is broken by an entrance on the SE side facing the fort. From the watch-tower the visitor can easily appreciate the purpose of the fort itself, a cork in the mouth of the Sma' Glen.

Some 18 km to the SW (and best reached from Crieff along the A85) was the fort of Dalginross (see Fig. 15), first surveyed by William Roy in 1755, at the head of Strathearn, on an extensive piece of flat ground with the mountains directly in front. The fort site (W of the B827 S of Comrie, by Ruchilhill farm) is partly eroded by the adjacent river, but its platform is easily made out, and a slight roll in the ground betrays the position of the ditches. Lying next to it (and straddling the modern road) was a 9.5 ha (23.5-acre) camp of the Stracathro type, also surveyed by Roy, relocated from the air. In 1990 its E gateway was explored in advance of a housing development. There is nothing Roman about the 'Roman Stone' beside the road, marked on OS maps.

Further again to the SW, at **Bochastle*** on the W outskirts of Callander, was another Highland Line fort, just below the Pass of Leny, where the River Teith emerges into open country. (Turn off the A84 2 km W of Callander on to the A821; just across the river turn into a carpark for the Trossachs National Park, and immediately left on to a rough track signposted for Bochastle farm; go as far as (but not under) the bridge below a long disused railway and climb on to the railway embankment for an elevated view of the fort which lies (on the right) between the embankment and the river.) The W rampart survives as a broad bank up to 2 m high, with a gap for the W gate. The N rampart has been eroded by the river, and the S rampart partly lost below the embankment, but the E rampart and ditches are visible. The fort was about 1.92 ha. (4.74 acres) in size; excavation in 1949 established a Flavian date, and showed that the site had suffered from flooding even in Roman times. On the S side of the fort were two camps, one with a 'Stracathro' gateway.

The next Highland Line fort was at Malling, on the SW shore of the Lake of Menteith, in the upper valley of the Forth, with the Menteith Hills and Ben Ledi rising sharply in front. The fort, which is of some 2.8 ha. (7 acres), with an annexe on the lochside, was found from the air in the later 1960s. Near to it were two camps, of which one has a Stracathro-type gate. (A short length of ditch belonging to the larger of the two camps survives next to a forestry plantation, but makes for a disappointing visit.) There is a fine view of the Lake from the jetty for Inchmahome Priory, at Port of Menteith.

Finally a fort lay near Drymen at Wester Drumquhassle farm close by the Endrick Water above Loch Lomond, on high ground with fine all-round views, bounded by mountains of the Highland massif on the N, the Kilpatrick Hills to the S, and on the SE by the distinctive summit of Dumgoyne at the end of the Campsie range. (Take a minor road eastwards from the A811, to follow what is now the route of the West Highland Way.) The fort was of about 1.43 ha. (3.2 acres); its ramparts are visible as a rather low mound, discernible only to the experienced observer. A further fort in the series, completing the cordon, could be looked for on the banks of the River Leven, at or near Dumbarton. The visitor who chooses to travel the route from Fendoch to Dumbarton in a day will gain an unparalleled insight into the geographical interface between the Romans and Caledonians on this 'far frontier'.

From the Tay to the North Esk

The fort at **Bertha**, the jumping-off point for Roman incursions into Strathmore, sat at the junction between the Tay and the Almond, 3 km north of Perth. (Take the A9, now bypassing Perth itself, to the Inveralmond roundabout, turn left to follow the A9, and after crossing the Almond, turn immediately left into a cul-de-sac. The fort lies in the field opposite, on the far side of the road, and is bisected by the railway. A faint ridge representing the N rampart lies almost directly ahead, faintly silhouetted against the railway embankment; a short length of what seems to be the S rampart survives in woodland overlooking the Almond on the margin of cultivated ground, beyond the railway line.) The fort was large, about 3.9 ha. (9.6 acres). In 1958 a dedication stone to *Discipulina Augusti*, the military discipline-cult favoured by emperors from Hadrian onwards, was recovered from the bed of the Almond nearby and is now in Perth Museum.

For Roman troops advancing NE from the Tay, two possible routes were available, either along the coast S of the Sidlaw Hills or through Strathmore following the Tay itself and its various tributaries to the

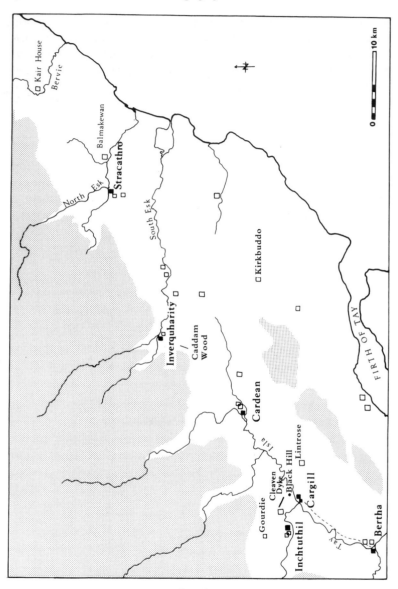

97. **Strathmore.**

NE. It is evident that the Roman army used both. Two series of camps, already referred to (above, p. 26), stand out, of 25 and 55 ha. (63 and 130 acres), evidently indicating the progress of particular task-forces, most probably in the Severan period. Just beyond Bertha, on the far side of the Tay, two such camps are known, at Scone and Grassy Walls, the former of 25 ha. and the latter of 55 ha. Some parts of the ramparts of the Grassy Walls camp are visible as faint mounds.

Impressive lengths of the rampart and ditch of a 25 ha. camp can be seen at **Kirkbuddo***, S of Forfar. (On the B9127, 5 km E of its junction with the A90; *c*.1 km E of the Whigstreet hamlet, the road veers to the left; park here on the right at a half-concealed wooden gate leading into woodland. On the opposite side of the road, 20 m E of the gate, is the bank of the camp-rampart.) The rampart, 1.5 m high with an accompanying ditch forming the W side of the camp, extends into the plantation for 300 m (Fig. 98). The rampart is broken by two gateways, each protected by a traverse *c*.15 m in front of the camp-ditch. The

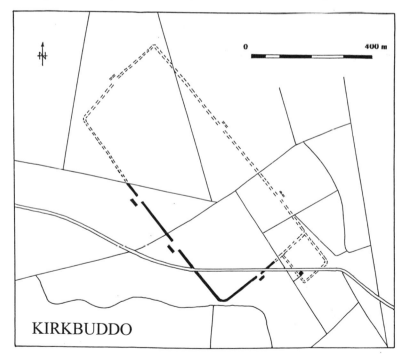

98. **Kirkbuddo, Angus:** ground-plan of the marching camp (after Crawford, with additions)

first gateway lies 100 m into the plantation, the second *c.*140 m further on; but it is obscured by trees. Both traverses are most impressive, consisting of a 12-m length of rampart fronted by a ditch of matching length. (Next return to the B9127, and cross it to visit the continuation of the W side of the camp, which can be followed to the SW corner and then along the S side; shortly before the B9127 again comes into view is another gateway, with traverse. From the modern road, look to either side *c.*100 m short of a house with high hedging at the edge of the woods.) A small annexe attached to the S side of the camp was planned by General Roy, but its defences are no longer visible.

On the line of the Tay itself (and this was evidently the chief route used by the Romans when this part of Scotland was occupied in the later first century AD), a fort and a fortlet lay close together at Cargill, south of the junction of the Tay and the Isla. The fortlet has been known since 1941; the fort (of 2.1 ha./5.2 acres) was located from the air in 1977. Both seem likely to belong in the Flavian period, given that the Romans do not seem to have established permanent forts N of the Tay in any other period, and from the few datable finds. A particular problem must be to relate them chronologically to the major site in the area, indeed the kingpin of the whole Flavian system in Scotland, the legionary fortress at **Inchtuthil**, barely 5 km distant to the NW.

The Inchtuthil fortress, first recognised as a major site in the 1750s, was examined in 1901 and comprehensively excavated in 1952–65; aerial reconnaisance over the years has added further details and confirmed the general correctness of the published plan which still forms the most completely known ground-plan of a single-period legionary fortress anywhere in the Roman Empire (Fig. 99; cf. Fig. 24). The fortress, of 21.7 ha. (53.5 acres), was abandoned while still under construction in about AD 86/87, when the occupying legion (probably the Twentieth) was moved to Chester, and the garrison of Britain substantially reduced.

The fortress lies N of a bend of the Tay between Meikleour, famous for its lofty beech hedge planted in 1746, and Caputh, some distance short of the Tay gorge at Dunkeld. (From the A984 W of Meikleour village, turn left on to a rough track signposted to Aird farm opposite the junction with the B947; continue to the far end of the track beside some cottages. The fortress lies on the plateau above, and is reached along a path leading uphill to the right of the cottages.) On the right of the path within a plantation of rhododendrons are the rampart

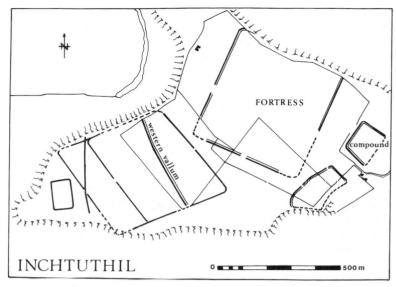

99. **Inchtuthil, Perth & Kinross:** ground-plan of the fortress and adjacent enclosures (after St Joseph). See Fig. 24 for a detailed plan of the fortress.

and defensive ditch of a rectangular enclosure, interpreted as a 'stores compound', now much overgrown. Some 100 m into the field beyond (beware of an electrified fence and, at times, a bull) is the broad E ditch of the fortress, which can be followed N (to the right) to an escarpment, on whose crest the N rampart lay (not now visible). The visitor should head W aiming for a white house in the distance, and just before a modern plantation bank he will encounter the fortress's W rampart, a broad low mound, running away to the left, its course marked by some trees. The accompanying W ditch can be followed towards the SW corner where the remains peter out in a cultivated field. An impressive length of the S defences, comprising rampart, berm and ditch, is visible in a patch of rough ground nearby. Looking back to the E rampart, the visitor will gain an impression of the area covered by the fortress.

Rather disappointingly perhaps, there is nothing to be seen in the interior of the site. The internal structures were timber-built, and included a headquarters building, hospital, workshop (from below the floor of which came the hoard of nearly 1,000,000 iron nails, many unused, left behind when the fortress was abandoned; Fig. 43), and 64 barracks. Occasional bumps and hollows in the interior are remnants of a golf course, long since disused. The rampart was initially of clay, but later received a stone revetment, left unfinished on the abandonment of the site. Close by, between the fortress and the end of the promontory on which it stands, was a labour camp and to the SE a temporary compound perhaps for officers, in use while the fortress was under construction. Ploughing has brought up debris from a bath-house which stood within the compound. Later, the whole promontory S of the fortress was cut off by the digging of a new rampart and ditch, the 'western vallum', of which some traces can be seen. (From the S rampart, walk NW along a field fence to reach a modern track; go left till a sharp dip marks the position of the Roman ditch which can be seen running off to the S.)

To the NW of Inchtuthil was a temporary camp at Gourdie. Within its limits is a group of large pits in the hillside, known locally as the 'Steed Stalls', a name which is sometimes applied to the site. It used to be thought that a quarry here produced building stone for the fortress's revetment wall, but the chief source of building stone is now known to lie some way to the W, and the date of the Steeds Stalls has been called into question. (To see the Steed Stalls, return from Inchtuthil to the A984, and go left, i.e. W, for 900 m, then to Middle Gourdie, then continue uphill on foot to the top of the ridge beside derelict buildings; look E to see the Steed Stalls as grassy hillocks in a planted field *c*.300 m downhill beyond a line of five trees. (The site can also be approached over flatter ground from the NE, from Hillocks of Gourdie farm.) The view from the hilltop towards Inchtuthil is not to be missed on a fine day, across Strathmore to the range of hills including Dunsinane, and those of Fife beyond.

Some 3 km E of Inchtuthil is a turf-reveted earthen bank flanked by shallow ditches which run in a straight line for some 2.25 km. It is known as the Cleaven Dyke. Its purpose and date were never clear; excavation followed by radiocarbon dating indicated that, instead of forming a boundary to the Roman site at Inchtuthil, as traditionally interpreted, it should be seen as a Neolithic 'cursus monument', dating to the mid-fourth millennium BC! (To see a length of the dyke, take the minor road signposted Lethendy just W of Meikleour village; after 1 km, before woodland terminates on the right, watch for a track leading away from the road; follow it until it cuts the prominent cambered mound of the dyke. Alternatively, the dyke can be seen to either side of the A93, 700 m N of its junction with the A984.) Formerly associated with the Cleaven Dyke, but now seen in its own right is a watch-tower, atop a natural hillock known as **Black Hill** (see Fig. 23). (Reached from the A984, 2 km E of its junction with the A93. Take the minor (unsignposted) road to Hallhole farm, asking there for access. Follow the track through the farm buildings until it turns sharply right. The watch-tower occupies the tree-covered hill beyond. Look for a path leading uphill. The OS 1:50,000 map may confuse the visitor; the 1:10,000 sheet shows the location of the site more clearly). Excavation in 1939 revealed a timber tower 3.5 m square within a rampart and a single ditch which still stands out clearly, along with a low mound representing the rampart and an upcast bank beyond. In the valley of the Isla, there is a camp of 25 ha. (63 acres) at Lintrose, 6 km E of Cargill; its once impressive ramparts have largely fallen victim to agricultural improvement, though a short stretch survives in woodland on the N edge of the hamlet of Campmuir.

Further along the valley of the Isla, which continues the line of the Tay to the NE, are a fort and two camps (the larger of 55 ha.) at **Cardean**, in the angle between the Isla and a tributary, the Dean Water. The fort belongs in the Flavian period; excavation in 1968–75 revealed a turf-built rampart with up to four external ditches; inside the fort the excavators located a timber-framed barrack block, a row of storerooms, and a granary; the foundation-trenches and pits for the major timber uprights showed up clearly in the yellow sandy subsoil. A resistivity survey in 2001 revealed many details including rampart-ovens, and caused the overall size of the fort to be reassessed, at 3.7 ha. (9.1 acres). Only the general outlines of the fort are now visible. (From the A94 outside Meigle – where there is a small museum housing Pictish Stones – to the NW, take the A927 for Alyth, then almost immediately a minor road signposted for Kirriemuir; soon after the road swings to the right to cross the Dean Water at a recent housing development, park at an inshot on the right-hand side of the road; the fort lies on the plateau beyond.). Some part of the defences of the 55 ha. camp survive in woodland, best accessed via an unsignposted road to Wester Cardean; continue beyond the farm. The S defences are in woodland to your left, *c.*60 m before the trees end; they become more visible 300 m into the wood.

The forts N from the Tay were linked by a road, following the line of the Isla. Just beyond Kirriemuir, in **Caddam Wood**, there is a fine stretch of cambered mound, though some scholars have questioned

100. **Stracathro, Angus:** aerial view of the Flavian fort (underlying the Church), seen from the NE, with an annexe and part of the marching camp beyond. (Photo: RCAHMS, Crown copyright). See also Fig. 14.

its Roman date. (Follow the B955 out of Kirriemuir to the NE, turn left into Mid Road, opposite a bus stop; park at the end of the lane on the edge of the wood, next to Woodside Cottage; pass through a modern gate into the woodland, and take the left hand of two available tracks; after *c.*50 m the cambered surface of the road comes into view on the right-hand side, flanked by drainage ditches. The mound is topped by a tree. It can be followed to the NE, where it is joined by a modern track which continues for 500 m through the wood.)

The line of Roman advance to the NE has always been supposed to cross the South Esk at Finavon, more or less on the line of the modern A90, where three camps are known, and a fort has been for some time postulated there. However, in 1983 aerial reconnaissance revealed a fortlet (or very small fort), not at the expected river crossing on the South Esk, but 8 km further W at Inverquharity Castle, near the junction of the South Esk with the Prosen Water and close to the mouths of Glen Clova and Glen Prosen, evidently overlying a native settlement; it has recently been the subject of a resistivity survey. A Flavian date can be presumed, and Inverquharity fortlet can be seen as another in the 'Highland Line' series, to be divorced from the group of camps further E on the South Esk, which are on the main line of Roman advance northwards. The road in Caddam Wood (above) heads towards Inverquharity, which should help to confirm its Roman origin. Further N at Stracathro, on the North Esk (where the river is joined from the W by two tributaries), lies what is currently the most northerly known fort in the Roman Empire, of some 2.6 ha. (6.4 acres), revealed initially by aerial reconnaissance (Fig. 100), and confirmed as of Flavian date by limited excavation in 1969. The site is partly covered by Stracathro Church and churchyard. (Turn off the A90 4 km N of Brechin signposted Inchbare, just before a service area and hospital; after crossing one of the tributaries, turn right at a T-junction, passing Smiddyhill farm, to reach Stracathro Church; park at the church gate.) The edge of the fort-platform on the SE side can be made out in the field opposite. Close by to the W is a marching camp of just under 15.7 ha. (40 acres), the type site of the Stracathro series (Fig. 14).

Aberdeenshire and the North

Beyond the North Esk no forts are securely known, but we should not suppose that Stracathro fort was necessarily the most northerly ever built in Scotland. Others may await detection from the air, perhaps at Fordoun on the Bervie Water, where there has been a long tradition of Roman earthworks, and near Stonehaven. Certainly the discovery of numerous camps over the years indicates the onward march of Roman armies beyond the North Esk. At first the camps lie at fairly regular intervals about 16 km apart, often at river crossings: Balmakewan on the far side of the North Esk (49.7 ha./123 acres), Kair House (52.6 ha./130 acres) on the Bervie Water; Raedykes (37.56 ha./ 93 acres), Normandykes on the Aberdeenshire Dee (43.3 ha./107 acres) and Kintore (44.5 ha./110 acres) at the crossing of the Don. The first two seem likely to belong to the series of 55-ha. camps which stretch northwards from Ardoch and may belong in the Severan age. But those beyond Stonehaven are smaller and it is tempting to see them as a separate group, perhaps marking the progress of Agricola himself. Some were noticed first by General Roy in the mid-eighteenth century, or were reported to him, though their defences have become less distinct over time; others were located by aerial photography. Two are well worth visiting: at **Raedykes*** almost the entire ditch circuit can

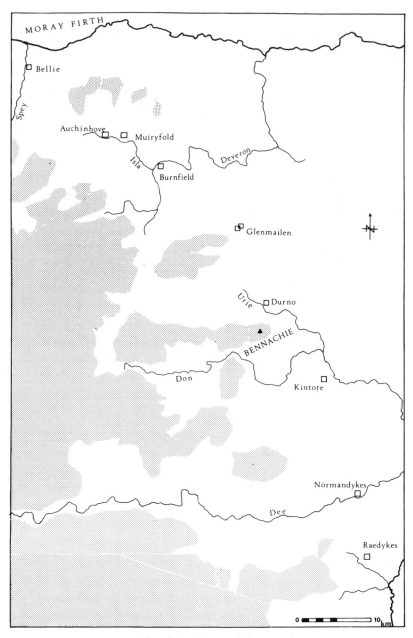

101. **Aberdeenshire and the North.**

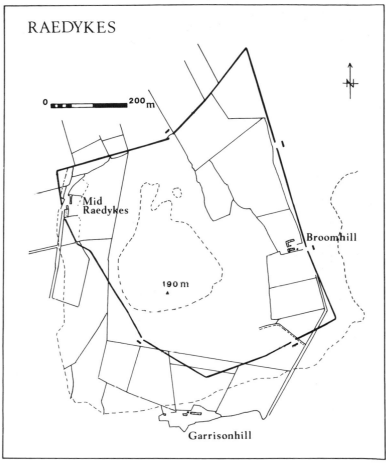

102. **Raedykes, Aberdeenshire:** ground-plan of the marching camp (after Macdonald).

be followed on the ground. (5 km NW of Stonehaven, turn N off the A957 on to a minor road, opposite a red postbox set in a stone wall, then fork right and where the road turns sharply right, go straight ahead on a track to Broomhill farm (see Fig. 102).) The E rampart stands up to 1 m high and *c.*3 m broad, with a ditch beyond still up to 1 m deep, with the gateways protected by traverses. The rampart should now be followed to the NE corner, where it turns sharply to the W. Here the defences are at their most impressive. The ditch can be followed for much of the rest of the camp's outline, except where it is faint on the S side. The ground is very uneven hereabouts, with a steep hill in the middle of the site, which may help to account for the irregularity of the outline. The chief reason for the selection of this site must have been the fine vista over the long stretch of coastline, with the harbour of Stonehaven in full view.

Part of the N side of the camp at **Normandykes** survives along the edge of a forestry plantation, with the rampart standing up to 2 m high, and the accompanying ditch 4 m wide. (At Peterculter on the A93 SW of Aberdeen, watch for a left turn signposted Kennerty, then passing through new housing to a farm, turn left after *c.*300 m on to a track leading to a disused railway line; park here and walk straight ahead to reach the plantation which stands clearly on the opposite slope; the nearer (left) corner of the plantation marks the NE angle of the Roman camp.)

Further N the line of Roman advance lay along the Don and subsequently its tributary, the River Urie. Recent excavation in advance of a housing development on the site of the camp at Kintore has revealed over more than 150 field-ovens, 35 rubbish or latrine pits, and numerous small finds, a guide to unexpectedly intensive activity in its interior; the date is as yet unclear.

At Durno near Pitcaple, 10 km NW of Inverurie, a camp of *c.*58 ha. (*c.*144 acres), was revealed from the air in 1977. Nothing is visible at ground level. Although this camp, the largest N of the Forth, is undated, a case was made out by Professor St Joseph for identifying it as Agricola's base on the eve of the battle of *Mons Graupius*, which he persuasively argued was fought out on the slopes of Bennachie, 5 km to the SW (above, p. 8). The conspicuous silhouette of Bennachie would make an excellent *Mons Graupius*, all but in sight of the 'end of Britain', as Tacitus reports. Although the camp at Durno is on the other side of the River Urie from Bennachie (Tacitus' account mentions no river barrier), it is sited at just a sufficient distance from the mountain to have discouraged any overnight raiding from a Caledonian host encamped on its slopes.

At the village of Oyne, 10 km W of Inverurie, is the Archaeolink Prehistory Park (signposted from the A96), with imaginative indoor displays illustrating the human history of the north-east from mesolithic hunter-gatherers to the Picts, and outdoor reconstructions of monuments and structures of various periods; the Roman interlude is represented by a line of tents within the defences of a segment of marching camp, the accommodation totally unappealing, especially on a wet day, by comparison with a nearby reconstructed Iron Age roundhouse. There are costumed interpreters and a programme of special events, which may feature Roman re-enactors (see below, p. 192).

Further to the NW two camps are known E of Huntly at **Glenmailen**. The defences of the larger camp of 44.9 ha. (111 acres) cut the rampart and ditch of the smaller which has a Stracathro-type gate. Evidently we have here evidence of two Roman armies, of greatly differing strength, using the same halting place. We could think of Agricolan forces in successive years (i.e. AD 82 and 83), unless this was an old Agricolan overnight encampment chosen again by Severus' army – all of 130 years later (!). The larger camp seems to belong with the group already mentioned (above, p. 183). (From the A96 23 km N of Inverurie go right on a minor road signposted to Wells of Ythan, then right again at road similarly signposted; then, after the hamlet itself, go right at a red telephone kiosk, signposted to Logie Newton; after 2 km Glenmellan [sic] farm comes into view on the left, with a large area of hard-standing in front. Cross the road, and then a dried-up stream bed to reach the site.) Part of the S rampart of the larger camp survives a field boundary SW of the farm, and other short stretches can with difficulty be pinpointed elsewhere along its circuit.

The rampart of the Glenmailen camp is the most northerly surviving Roman earthwork visible in Britain, but beyond Glenmailen a further camp has been tentatively identified at Burnfield near Milltown on the River Deveron. Two more camps, located by aerial photography in the 1950s, lie close together near Keith, at Muiryfold and Auchinhove, where the River Isla negotiates the Pass of Grange. The camp at Auchinhove, of 12 ha. (30 acres), has Stracathro-type gates, and must be assigned to the Flavian period. The larger is of 44 ha. (109 acres). Here two task-forces have stopped at much the same halting place, a day's northwards march beyond Glenmailen. Some 20 km beyond there is a possible camp (never confirmed as Roman by excavation) at Bellie NW of Fochabers, on a plateau above the flood-plain of the Spey at a point long used as a crossing over the river – it was here that part of the Duke of Cumberland's army crossed the Spey on its march to Culloden in 1746. That this camp (if confirmed) should mark the limit of Roman advances in Scotland must be highly unlikely; certainly a further day's march would bring an army to Burghead, later an important Pictish fort. It is tempting to see in Burghead the *Pinnata Castra* (the 'winged' or 'battlemented camp') mentioned by Ptolemy, as lying on or near the Spey. In 2000 and 2001 coin hoards datable to the Severan period were revealed buried below floors in an Iron Age homestead site at Birnie near Elgin, part of a large settlement occupied over a long period before and after the Roman interlude. It seems natural to interpret these coins as among the subsidies which we know were paid by the Romans to native chiefs in north Britain at this time (above, p. 54).

Aerial photography by the late Professor G.D.B. Jones identified several possible Roman sites between Forres and Inverness, which were tested by excavation: at Easter Galcantray, near Cawdor, the foundations of timber-framed buildings, reminiscent of Roman workmanship, were examined, but Roman small finds were lacking to confirm the date. However, the idea of permanent installations N of the Grampians should not be too hastily rejected. Both Agricola and Severus are said to have reached the far end of Britain; whether such statements should be interpreted literally is for future researchers to determine.

APPENDIX 1

Museums in Scotland with Roman Displays

Intending visitors are advised to check opening hours with individual museums, by telephone or on their websites. Many museums stock leaflets, guidebooks, slides and activity sheets for school pupils or teachers' packs with a Roman theme.

Annan Annan Museum, Bank St. (Wed.–Sat., 11 a.m.–4 p.m.) Attractive new displays, including some finds from Birrens, aerial photographs of local sites, replicas of an altar (here Fig. 31) and of a relief sculpture of Brigantia (here Fig. 32), a reconstruction of the 'chapel of the standards' at Birrens; children's activities; occasional 'Roman days'. Webpages: www.annan.org.uk. Tel: 01461 201384.

Biggar Moat Park Heritage Centre, Kirkstyle (Easter–October: Mon.–Sat., 10 a.m.–5 p.m.; Sun., 2–5 p.m.) Finds from Castledykes and imaginative displays on the Romans in Clydesdale. Webpages: www. biggar-net.co.uk/museums. Tel: 01899 221050.

Bo'ness Kinneil Museum, Kinneil Estate (Mon.–Sat., 12.30–4 p.m.) Finds from nearby Kinneil fortlet; altar from Westerwood fort. Webpages: falkirkmuseums.demon.co.uk/museums/kinnmus. Tel: 01506 778530.

Dumfries Dumfries Museum, The Observatory (April–September: Mon–Sat., 10 a.m.–5 p.m.; Sun., 2–5 p.m.; October–March: Tues.–Sat., 10 a.m.–1 p.m., 2 p.m.–5 p.m.) Finds, especially small bronzes, from Carzield, Burnswark, Birrens, Dalswinton, Glenlochar and other sites in SW Scotland; good aerial photographs of local sites. Altars and a tombstone from Birrens are in the 'sacred stones' room on the lowest floor of the 'camera obscura', originally a windmill. Webpages: www. dumgall.gov.uk. Tel: 01387 253374.

Dundee McManus Galleries, Albert Square (Mon.–Sat., 10 a.m.–5 p.m.; Thurs., 10 a.m.–7 p.m.; Sun., 12.30–4 p.m.) Material from Carpow, including fragments of commemorative slabs. Webpages: www.dundeecity.gov.uk. Tel: 01382 432084.

Edinburgh Museum of Scotland, Chambers St. (Mon., Wed.–Sat., 10 a.m.–5 p.m.; Tues., 10 a.m.–8 p.m.; Sun., 12 noon–5 p.m.) Major permanent display, integrated thematically within the 'Early Peoples of Scotland' exhibition, including many altars, Bridgeness distance slab, sculptures and spectacular small finds from numerous sites, including Newstead, Birrens, Rough Castle and Mumrills. Also 'Traprain Treasure,' Cramond Lioness, Helmsdale Hoard, and Deskford carnyx. Webpages: www.nms.ac.uk. Tel: 0131 247 4422.

Edinburgh Museum of Edinburgh, Huntly House, 142 Canongate (June–September: Mon.–Sat., 10 a.m.–5 p.m.; Sun., during August, 2–5 p.m.) A few finds from Cramond fort. Wepages: www.cac.org.uk. Tel: 0131 529 4143.

Glasgow Hunterian Museum, University of Glasgow (Mon.–Sat., 9.30 a.m.-5 p.m.) Major permanent display of material from Antonine Wall and sites in SW Scotland, including numerous distance slabs, and many small finds from forts at Bar Hill, Bearsden, Castledykes, Loudoun Hill and elsewhere; Coin Gallery. Webpages: www.hunterian. gla.ac.uk. Tel: 0141 330 4221.

Glasgow Art Gallery and Museum, Kelvingrove. Closed for refurbishment until early 2006. Local material, replicas, fort-models and one distance slab may be incorporrated in new theme-based displays. Webpages: g3web.co.uk/glasgow_museums/art-gallery/ index.htm. Tel: 0141 287 2699.

Kirkintilloch Auld Kirk Museum, Cowgate (Tues.–Sat., 10 a.m.– 1 p.m., 2–5 p.m.) Some finds from Bar Hill, in an attractive new display. Webpages: www.eastdunbarton.gov.uk. Tel: 0141 578 0144

Melrose The 'Three Hills' Roman Heritage Centre, Ormiston Insitute, Market Sq. (1 April–31 October daily 10.30 a.m.–4.30 p.m.; closed Sat., Sun., 1–2 p.m. During the winter months may be opened on request.) The history and interpretation of Newstead fort and environs; numerous finds by arrangement with the National Museums of Scotland; weekly walks (Thursday p.m.). Webpages: www.trimontium.freeserve.co.uk. Tel: 01896 822651.

Melrose Abbey Museum (April–September: daily 9.30 a.m.– 6.30 p.m.; October–March: Mon.–Sat., 9.30 a.m.–4.30 p.m.; Sun., 2–4.30 p.m.) One room of the Commendator's House contains finds from Newstead. Webpages: www.historic-Scotland.gov.uk.

Perth Museum and Art Gallery, 78 George St. (Mon.–Sat., 10 a.m.–
5 p.m.) Archaeological material, including an inscribed stone from
Bertha, has been incorporated in a thematic display on local history.
Webpages: www.pkc.gov.uk/ah/perth_museum. Tel: 01738 632488.

Selkirk Halliwell's House, Halliwell's Close (April–September:
Mon.– Sat., 10 a.m.–5 p.m.; Sun., 10 a.m.– 12 p.m; July–August:
Mon.–Sat., 10 a.m.–5.30 p.m.; Sun., 2–5 p.m.; October: Mon.–Sat.,
10 a.m.– 4 p.m.) Small display of finds from Newstead; timber upright
from Oakwood fort. Webpages: www.discovertheborders/places/71.
htm. Tel: 01750 20096.

In addition, small collections of Roman material are held in several
other museums, including Aberdeen (Marischal Museum), Clydebank,
Cumbernauld, Forfar, Galashiels, Hawick, Kilmarnock, Montrose
and Stirling, where they may form part of special exhibitions.

APPENDIX 2

USEFUL WEBSITES

Archaeolink Prehistory Park, Oyne, Inverurie, Aberdeenshire. Webpages: www.archaeolink.co.uk. Tel: 01464 851500.

Antonine Guard www.theantonineguard.org.uk

Brigantium museums.ncl.ac.uk/wallnet/brig. Tel: 01830 520801

Britannia Roman Sites www.morgue.demon.co.uk.

Council for Scottish Archaeology www.britarch.ac.uk/csa. Tel: 0131 247 4119

Historic Scotland www.historic-scotland.gov.uk. Tel: 0131 668 8777

RCAHMS www.rcahms.gov.uk. Tel: 0131 662 1456

Roman Gask Project www.morgue.demon.co.uk/pages/Gask

SCRAN www.scran.ac.uk. Tel: 0131 662 1211

Society for the Promotion of Roman Studies www.romansociety. org.uk Tel: 0207 862 8727

Trimontium Trust www.trimontium.freeserve.co.uk. Tel: 0189 682 2651

BIBLIOGRAPHY

Only a selection of the available general works can be noticed here, and for individual sites reference has been made only to major excavation reports and to recent discoveries, if any. The results of recent archaeological activity will be found in *Discovery and Excavation in Scotland*, published annually by the Council for Scottish Archaeology (CSA) and in the journal *Britannia*, published annually by the Society for the Promotion of Roman Studies, London.

The Bibliography is subdivided according to the chapter headings used in the foregoing pages. For Part 2, the archaeological sites mentioned in each chapter are listed alphabetically except that the Gask Ridge watch-towers are considered as a single group. The letters and numerals after each site-name are its National Grid Reference, which should ease their identification on OS maps.

Abbreviations used

DES	*Discovery and Excavation in Scotland*
GAJ	*Glasgow Archaeological Journal*
JRS	*Journal of Roman Studies*
PSAS	*Proceedings of the Society of Antiquaries of Scotland*
ROSWS	*The Roman Occupation of South-Western Scotland*, ed. S.N. Miller (Glasgow, 1952)
SAJ	*Scottish Archaeological Journal*
TDGNHAS	*Transactions of the Dumfriesshire and Galloway Natural History and Antiquarian Society*
TGAS	*Transactions of the Glasgow Archaeological Society*
TRSNAW	*Topography of Roman Scotland North of the Antonine Wall*, O.G.S. Crawford (Cambridge, 1949)

PART 1

Scotland on the eve of the Roman Invasion

I. Armit, *Celtic Scotland* (London, 1997)
R. Cunliffe, *The extraordinary Voyage of Pytheas the Greek* (London, 2001)

R. Hingley, *Settlement and Sacrifice: The Later Prehistoric People of Scotland* (Edinburgh, 1998)

I.A. Richmond (ed.), *Roman and Native in North Britain* (Edinburgh, 1958)

G. and A. Ritchie, *Scotland: Archaeology and Early History* (London, 1981)

A.L.F. Rivet (ed.), *The Iron Age in Northern Britain* (Edinburgh, 1967)

The Romans in Scotland: an Historical Outline

A.R. Birley, *Septimius Severus: The African Emperor* (London, 1971; 2nd ed., 1999)

A.R. Birley, *Tacitus: Agricola, Germany* (Oxford, 1999)

A. Breeze, 'Philology on Tacitus' Graupian Hill and Trucculan harbour', *PSAS* 132 (2002), 305–11

D.J. Breeze, *The Northern Frontiers of Roman Britain* (London, 1982; 2nd ed., 1993)

D.J. Breeze, 'Why did the Romans fail to conquer Scotland?', *PSAS* 118 (1988), 3–22

D.J. Breeze, 'Agricola in the Highlands', *PSAS* 120 (1990), 55–60

D.J. Breeze, *Roman Scotland: Frontier Country* (London, 1996)

D.J. Breeze, 'The great myth of Caledon', in T.C. Smout (ed.), *Scottish Woodland History* (Edinburgh, 1997), 47–51

D.J. Breeze, 'The edge of the world: the imperial frontier and beyond', in P. Salway (ed.), *The Short Oxford History of the British Isles: The Roman Era* (Oxford, 2002), 173–200

D.J. Breeze and B. Dobson, *Hadrian's Wall* (Harmondsworth, 1976; 4th ed., 2000)

A.R. Burn, *Agricola and Roman Britain* (London, 1953)

A.P. Fitzpatrick, 'The submission of the Orkney Islands to Claudius: new evidence?', *Scott. Arch. Review* 6 (1989), 24–33

S.S. Frere, *Britannia: A History of Roman Britain* (London, 1967; revised 3rd ed., 1999)

W.S. Hanson, *Agricola and the Conquest of the North* (London, 1987)

W.S. Hanson, 'Scotland and the Northern Frontier: second to fourth centuries AD', in M. Todd (ed.), *A Companion to Roman Britain* (Oxford, 2004), 136–61

W.S. Hanson and D.J. Breeze, 'The future of Roman Scotland', in W.S. Hanson and E.A. Slater (eds), *Scottish Archaeology: new Perspectives* (Aberdeen, 1991), 57–80

W.S. Hanson and G.S. Maxwell, Rome's *North-West Frontier: the Antonine Wall* (Edinburgh, 1986)

B.R. Hartley, 'The Roman Occupations of Scotland: the evidence of samian ware', *Britannia* 3 (1972), 1–45

A.S. Hobley, 'The numismatic evidence for the post-Agricolan abandonment of the Roman frontier in northern Scotland', *Britannia* 20 (1989), 69–74

N. Hodgson, 'Were there two Antonine occupations of Scotland?', *Britannia* 26 (1995), 29–49

J.G.F. Hind, 'Caledonia and its occupation under the Flavians', *PSAS* 113 (1983), 373–78

B. Hoffman, 'Tacitus, *Agricola* and the role of literature in the archaeology of the first century AD', in E.W. Sauer (ed.), *Archaeology and Ancient History: Breaking down the Boundaries* (London, 2004), 151–65

J. Kenworthy (ed.), 'The Scottish Campaigns of Agricola', *Scottish Archaeological Forum* 12, 1980 (Edinburgh, 1981)

G. Macdonald, *The Roman Wall in Scotland* (Glasgow, 1911; 2nd ed., Oxford, 1934)

J.C. Mann, 'The Northern Frontier after AD 369', *GAJ* 3 (1974), 34–42

G.S. Maxwell, 'Sidelight on the Roman military campaigns in North Britain', in *Studien zu den Militärgrenzen Roms* III (Stuttgart, 1986), 60–63

G.S. Maxwell, *A Battle Lost: Romans and Caledonians at Mons Graupius* (Edinburgh, 1989)

G.S. Maxwell, *The Romans in Scotland* (Edinburgh, 1989)

G.S. Maxwell, 'Flavian frontiers in Caledonia', in H. Vetters and M. Kandler (eds), *Akten des 14. internationalen Limeskongresses 1986 in Carnuntum* (Vienna, 1990), 353–65

G.S. Maxwell, *A Gathering of Eagles: Scenes from Roman Scotland* (Edinburgh, 1998)

G.S. Maxwell, 'The Roman penetration of the north in the late first century AD', in M. Todd (ed.), *A Companion to Roman Britain* (Oxford, 2004), 75–90

R.M. Ogilvie and I.A. Richmond, *Cornelii Taciti de Vita Agricolae* (Oxford, 1967)

A. Ritchie and D.J. Breeze, *Invaders of Scotland* (Edinburgh, 1991)

A.S. Robertson, *The Antonine Wall* (Glasgow, 1960; 5th ed., 2001)

D.J. Robinson, 'The Romans and Ireland again: some thoughts on

Tacitus' Agricola Chapter, 24', *Journ. Chester Arch. Soc.* 75 (1998–99), 19–31

D.C.A. Shotter, 'Petillius Cerealis in Northern Britain', *Northern History* 36.2 (2000), 189–98

I.G. Smith, *The First Roman Invasion of Scotland* (Edinburgh, 1987)

P. Southern, 'Men and mountains, or geographical determinism and the conquest of Scotland', *PSAS* 126 (1986), 371–86

J.K. St Joseph, 'The camp at Durno, Aberdeenshire, and the Site of Mons Graupius', *Britannia* 9 (1978), 271–87

A. Strang, 'Recreating a possible Flavian map of Roman Britain, with a detailed map of Scotland', *PSAS* 128 (1998), 425–40

L. Thoms (ed.), 'The Romans in Scotland', *Scottish Archaeological Forum* 7, 1975 (Edinburgh, 1976)

M. Todd, *Roman Britain 55 BC – AD 400* (London, 1981; 3rd ed., 1999)

R.B. Warner, 'Tuathal Techtmar: a myth or ancient literary evidence for a Roman invasion [of Ireland]', *Emania* 13 (1995), 23–32

D.J. Woolliscroft, 'More thoughts on why the Romans failed to conquer Scotland', *SAJ* 22.2 (2000), 111–22

The Roman Army in Britain

A.R. Birley, 'Officers of the Second Augustan Legion', *Third Annual Caerleon Lecture* (Cardiff, 1990)

E. Birley, 'The fate of the Ninth Legion', in R.M. Butler (ed.), *Soldier and Civilian in Roman Yorkshire* (Leicester, 1971), 71–80

D.J. Breeze, 'The Second Augustan Legion in North Britain', *Second Annual Caerleon Lecture* (Cardiff, 1989)

R. Brewer (ed.), *The Second Augustan Legion and the Roman Military Machine* (Cardiff, 2002)

R.W. Davies, *Service in the Roman Army*, ed. D.J. Breeze and V.A. Maxfield (Edinburgh/Durham, 1989)

P.A. Holder, *The Roman Army in Britain* (London, 1982)

M.G. Jarrett, 'Non-legionary troops in Roman Britain: Part 1, the Units', *Britannia* 25 (1994), 35–77

G. Webster, *The Roman Imperial Army* (Edinburgh, 1969; 3rd ed., revised by H. Elton, 1998)

Roman Military Installations

P. Bidwell, *Roman Forts in Britain* (London, 1997)

H. Davies, *Roads in Roman Britain* (Stroud, 2002)

A. Graham and I.A. Richmond, 'Roman communications in the Tweed Valley', *PSAS* 87 (1952–53), 63–71

A. Johnson, *Roman Forts of the 1st and 2nd centuries AD in Britain and the German Provinces* (London, 1983)

I.D. Margary, *Roman Roads in Britain* (London, 1973)

G.S. Maxwell, 'The evidence from the Roman Period', in A. Fenton and G. Stell (eds), *Loads and Roads in Scotland and Beyond* (Edinburgh, 1984), 21–48

T.H. Rowland, *Dere Street: Roman Road North* (Newcastle, 1974)

R. Selkirk, *The Piercebridge Formula* (Cambridge, 1983)

The Monuments in the Landscape

O.G.S. Crawford, *Topography of Roman Scotland North of the Antonine Wall* (Cambridge, 1949)

S.N. Miller (ed.), *The Roman Occupation of South-Western Scotland* (Glasgow, 1952)

Piecing Together the Roman Past

D.J. Breeze, 'Demand and supply on the northern frontier', in R. Miket and C. Burgess (eds), *Between and Beyond the Walls: Essays on the Prehistory and History of North Britain* (Edinburgh, 1984), 264–86

D.J. Breeze, 'The manufacture of pottery in Roman Scotland', *PSAS* 126 (1986), 185–89

A.R. Burn, *The Romans in Britain: an Anthology of Inscriptions* (Oxford, 1969)

R.G. Collingwood and I. A. Richmond, *The Archaeology of Roman Britain* (London, 1969)

R.G. Collingwood and R. P. Wright (eds), *The Roman Inscriptions of Britain*, vol. 1 (Oxford, 1965; 2nd ed., Stroud, 1995), vol. 2 (Stroud, 1990–95)

S.S. Frere and J.K.S. St Joseph, *Roman Britain from the Air* (Cambridge, 1983)

L. Keppie, 'The Romans in Southern Scotland: future discoveries', *GAJ* 16 (1989–90), 1–28

L. Keppie, *Understanding Roman Inscriptions* (London, 1991; repr. 2001)

L. Keppie, *Roman Inscribed and Sculptured Stones in the Hunterian Museum, University of Glasgow* (London, 1998)

L.J.F. Keppie and B.J. Arnold, *Corpus of Sculpture of the Roman World (Corpus Signorum Imperii Romani)*, vol. 1, fasc. 4 (*Scotland*) (London, 1984)

J. Liversidge, *Britain in the Roman Empire* (London, 1968)

G.S. Maxwell and D.R. Wilson, 'Air Reconnaissance in Roman Britain, 1977–84', *Britannia* 18 (1987), 1–48

A.L.F. Rivet and C. Smith, *The Place-Names of Roman Britain* (London, 1979)

A.S. Robertson, 'Roman Finds from non-Roman Sites in Scotland', *Britannia* 1 (1970), 198–226

A.S. Robertson, 'The Romans in North Britain: The coin evidence', in H. Temporini and W. Haase (eds), *Aufstieg und Niedergang der römischen Welt*, II.3 (Berlin-New York, 1975), 364–426

A.S. Robertson, 'The circulation of Roman coins in North Britain: the evidence of hoards and site-finds from Scotland', in R.A.G. Carson and C.M. Kraay (eds.), *Scripta Nummaria Romana* (London, 1978), 186–216

A.S. Robertson, *An Inventory of Romano-British Coin Hoards* (London, 2000)

J.K.S. St Joseph, 'Aerial Reconnaissance of Roman Scotland, 1939–75', *GAJ* 4 (1975), 1–28

The Rediscovery of Roman Scotland

I.G. Brown, *The Hobby-Horsical Antiquary* (Edinburgh, 1981)

Glasgow Archaeological Society, *The Antonine Wall Report* (Glasgow, 1899)

A. Gordon, *Itinerarium Septentrionale* (London, 1726)

J. Horsley, *Britannia Romana* (London, 1732)

W. Maitland, *History and Antiquities of Scotland* (London, 1757)

W. Roy, *Military Antiquities of the Romans in Britain* (London, 1793)

R. Sibbald, *Historical Inquiries* (London, 1707)

R. Stuart, *Caledonia Romana* (Edinburgh, 1844; 2nd ed., 1852)

R. Sweet, *Antiquaries: the Discovery of the Past in Eighteenth-Century Britain* (London, 2004)

University of Glasgow, *Monumenta Romani Imperii* (Glasgow, 1768; 2nd ed., 1792)

Life on the Frontier

A.R. Birley, *Garrison Life at Vindolanda: a Band of Brothers* (London, 2002)

A.K. Bowman, *Life and Letters on the Roman Frontier: Vindolanda and its People* (London, 1994)

D.V. Clarke, D.J. Breeze and G. Mackay, *The Romans in Scotland* (Edinburgh, 1980)

P. Salway, *The Frontier People of Roman Britain* (Cambridge, 1965)

The Impact of Rome

I. Armit, 'The abandonment of souterrains: evolution, catastrophe or dislocation', *PSAS* 129 (1999), 577–96

D.J. Breeze, 'Roman forces and native populations', *PSAS* 115 (1985), 223–28

C. Dickson and J.F. Dickson, *Plants and People in Ancient Scotland* (Stroud, 2000)

K.J. Edwards and I. Ralston, *Scotland: Environment and Archaeology, 8000 BC–AD 1000* (Chichester, 1997)

W.S. Hanson, 'Forest clearance and the Roman army', *Britannia* 27 (1996), 354–58

R. Hingley, 'Society in Scotland from 700 BC to AD 200', *PSAS* 122 (1992), 7–53

R. Hingley, 'Rural settlement in Northern Britain', in M. Todd (ed.), *A Companion to Roman Britain* (Oxford, 2004), 327–48

F. Hunter, 'Roman and native in Scotland: new approaches', *Journal of Roman Archaeology* 14 (2001), 289–309

L. Keppie, 'Beyond the northern frontier: Roman and native in Scotland', in M. Todd (ed.), *Research on Roman Britain 1960–89* (London, 1989), 61–73

L. Keppie and S. Bryson, 'Pontius Pilate: the Scottish connection', *Archaeo: Current Research, Archaeology, Classics, Ancient History in Scotland* 2 (1994), 37–44

L. Macinnes, 'Brochs and the Roman occupation of Lowland Scotland,' *PSAS* 114 (1984), 235–49

R. Miket and C. Burgess (eds), *Between and Beyond the Walls* (Edinburgh, 1984)

H.H. Scullard, *Roman Britain: Outpost of the Empire* (London, 1979)

M. Todd, 'The Falkirk hoard of denarii: trade or subsidy', *PSAS* 115 (1985), 229–32

J. Wacher, *The Coming of Rome* (London, 1979)

G. Whittington and K.J. Edwards, 'Ubi solitudinem faciunt pacem appellant: the Romans in Scotland, a palaeo-environmental contribution', *Britannia* 24 (1993), 13–25

A. Wilson, 'Roman penetration of Strathclyde South of the Antonine Wall, part 1: The topographical framework', *GAJ* 19 (1994–95), 1–30

A. Wilson, 'Roman penetration of Strathclyde South of the Antonine Wall, part 2: 'Romanization', *GAJ* 20 (1996–97), 1–40

A. Wilson, 'Roman penetration in Eastern Dumfriesshire and Beyond', *TDGNHAS* 73 (1999), 17–62

A. Wilson, 'The Novantae and Romanisation in Galloway', *TDGNHAS* 75 (2001), 73–131

A. Wilson, 'Roman and native in Dumfriesshire', *TDGNHAS* 77 (2003), 103–60

PART 2

General

D.J. Breeze, *Roman Scotland: a Guide to the Visible Remains* (Newcastle, 1979)

S.S. Frere, A.L.F. Rivet and N.H.H. Sitwell, *Tabula Imperi Romani, Britannia Septentrionalis* (London, 1987)

Ordnance Survey, *Map of Roman Britain* (4th ed., HMSO 1991)

Ordnance Survey, *Map of the Antonine Wall* (HMSO 1969)

R. J. A. Wilson, *A Guide to the Roman Remains in Britain* (London, 1975; 4th ed., 2002)

Scotland South of the Antonine Wall

General (including roads): S.N. Miller (ed.), *The Roman Occupation of South-Western Scotland* (Glasgow, 1952); Royal Commission on the Ancient and Historical Monuments of Scotland (RCAHMS), Inventories: *Dumfriesshire* (Edinburgh, 1920), *Midlothian and West Lothian* (Edinburgh, 1929), *Peeblesshire* (Edinburgh, 1967), *Selkirkshire* (Edinburgh, 1957), *Roxburghshire* (Edinburgh, 1956); RCAHMS, *Eastern Dumfriesshire: an Archaeological Landscape* (Edinburgh,

1997); RCAHMS, Exploring Scotland's Heritage: G. Stell, *Dumfries and Galloway* (Edinburgh, 1996), J. R. Baldwin, *Edinburgh, Lothians and the Borders* (Edinburgh, 1997), J. Stevenson, *Glasgow, Clydeside and Stirling* (Edinburgh, 1995), B. Walker, *Fife, Perthshire and Angus* (Edinburgh, 1996).

Bankhead (NS 971449) *Britannia* 15 (1984), 265

Barburgh Mill (NX 902884) D.J. Breeze, *Britannia* 5 (1974), 130–62

Barnhill (NX 085028) T. Neighbour, I. Armit, B. Finlayson, I. Ralston, *TDGNHAS* 69 (1994), 7–12; *Britannia* 26 (1995), 337

Barochan (NS 413690) L.J.F. Keppie and F. Newall, *GAJ* 20 (1996–97), 41–76

Beattock Summit (NS 999153) G.S. Maxwell, *Britannia* 7 (1976), 33–38

Birrens (NY 219752) A.S. Robertson, *Birrens (Blatobulgium)* (Edinburgh 1975); C.E. Lowe, *TDGNHAS* 66 (1991), 11–35; idem, *Current Archaeology* 135, August/September 1993), 88–92; L.J.F. Keppie, *TDGNHAS* 69 (1994), 35–51; *Britannia* 28 (1997), 410; F.J. Hunter and I.G. Scott, *TDGNHAS* 76 (2002), 79–90

Bishopton (NS 418720) K.A. Steer, *PSAS* 83 (1948–49), 28–32; F. Newall, *Scottish Naturalist* 109 (1997), 55–96; ibid. 110 (1998), 13–43

Bothwellhaugh (NS 731577) J. Macdonald, *TGAS* n.s. 2 (1888–95), 312–23; RCAHMS, *Lanarkshire*, 119–21; L.J.F. Keppie, *GAJ* 8 (1981), 46–94

Broomholm (NY 378814) R.W. Feachem, *TDGNHAS* 28 (1949–50), 188–89; *JRS* 52 (1962), 164; 53 (1963),128; 55 (1965), 202

Brownhart Law (NT 790096) J.K. St Joseph, *PSAS* 83 (1948–49), 170–74; RCAHMS, *Roxburghshire*, 378–79

Burnswark (NY 186787) D. Christison, J. Barbour, J. Anderson, *PSAS* 33 (1898–99), 198–249; G. Jobey, *TDGNHAS* 53 (1977–78), 57–104; D.B. Campbell, *Britannia* 34 (2003), 19–33

Cappuck (NT 695212) I.A. Richmond, *PSAS* 85 (1950–51), 138–45; RCAHMS, *Roxburghshire*, 381–83

Carronbridge (NX 868977) D.A. Johnston, *PSAS* 124 (1994), 233–91

Carzield (NX 968818) E. Birley and I.A. Richmond, *TDGNHAS* 22 (1938–39), 156–63; E. Birley and J.P. Gillam, ibid. 24 (1945–46), 69–78; *DES* 1956, 14

Castledykes (NS 929442) A.S. Robertson, *The Roman Fort at Castledykes* (Edinburgh, 1964); RCAHMS, *Lanarkshire*, 124–28; L. Keppie, *GAJ* 19 (1994–95), 75–81

Castle Greg (NT 050592) RCAHMS, *Midlothian and West Lothian*, 140; *Britannia* 20 (1989), 271

Channelkirk (NT 473548) J.K. St Joseph, *JRS* 51 (1961), 121

Chew Green (NT 788084) I.A. Richmond and G.S. Keeney, *Archaeologia Aeliana* ser. 4, 14 (1937), 129–50; I.A. Richmond, 'The Romans in Redesdale', *Northumberland County History* 15 (Newcastle, 1940), 63–159; H. Welfare and V. Swan, *Roman Camps in England* (London, 1995), 85–90

Cleghorn (NS 910459) RCAHMS, *Lanarkshire*, 128

Craik Cross (NT 303047) I.A. Richmond, *PSAS* 80 (1945–6), 103–17; J.K. St Joseph, *TDGNHAS* 24 (1945–46), 151; RCAHMS, *Roxburghshire*, 402–3

Cramond (NT 189768) A. and V. Rae, *Britannia* 5 (1974), 163–224; M. Collard and F. Hunter, *PSAS* 130 (2000), 525–35; N. Holmes, *Excavation of Roman Sites at Cramond*, ed. M. Collard and J.A. Lawson (Edinburgh, 2003); frequent reports of work in *DES* and *Britannia*. Lioness sculpture: F. Hunter and M. Collard, *Current Archaeology* 155 (Dec. 1997), 404–07; M. Collard, *Pax Romana: the Cramond Lioness* (Edinburgh, 1998)

Crawford (NS 953214) G.S. Maxwell, *PSAS* 104 (1971–72), 147–200; RCAHMS, *Lanarkshire*, 128–33

Crichton (NT 400619) H. Welfare in C. Burgess and R. Miket (eds), *Between and Beyond the Walls* (Edinburgh, 1984), 305–23; L. Keppie, *GAJ* 16 (1989–90), 13

Dalmakethar (NY 107924) S.N. Miller, *ROSWS*, 101–3

Dalswinton (NX 933848) I.A. Richmond and J.K. St Joseph, *TDGNHAS* 34 (1955–56), 9–21; E. Birley, ibid., 35 (1956–57), 9–13

Drumlanrig (NX 854989) *Britannia* 16 (1985), 267; G.S. Maxwell and D.R. Wilson, *Britannia* 18 (1987), 19

Durisdeer (NS 903049) S.N. Miller, *ROSWS*, 124–26

Easter Happrew (NT 194401) K.A. Steer, *PSAS* 90 (1956–57), 93–101; RCAHMS, *Peeblesshire*, 169–71

Easter Langlee (NT 520361) K.A. Steer, *PSAS* 98 (1964–66), 320–21

Eildon Hill North (NT 554328) K.A. Steer and R.W. Feachem, *PSAS* 86 (1951–52), 202–5; RCAHMS, *Roxburghshire*, 306–10

Elginhaugh (NT 321673) G.S. Maxwell, *Britannia* 14 (1983), 167–81; G.S. Maxwell and D.R. Wilson, *Britannia* 18 (1987), 18; W. S. Hanson and P.A. Yeoman, *Elginhaugh* (Edinburgh, 1988)

Ewes Doors (NY 372986) *Britannia* 28 (1997), 410

Gatehouse of Fleet (NX 595575) J.K. St Joseph, in B.R. Hartley and J. Wacher (eds), *Rome and her Northern Provinces* (Gloucester, 1983), 222–34

Gilnockie (NY 389792) RCAHMS, *Dumfriesshire*, 27–28

Girvan (NX 191991) J.K. St Joseph, *Britannia* 9 (1978), 397–401; *Britannia* 25 (1994), 257

Glenlochar (NX 735645) I.A. Richmond and J.K. St Joseph, *TDGNHAS* 30 (1951–52), 1–16

Glenluce (NX 196566) *Britannia* 24 (1993), 281

Inveresk (NT 342720) I.A. Richmond, *PSAS* 110 (1978–80), 286–304; W.S. Hanson, *PSAS* 114 (1984), 251–59; G. Thomas, *PSAS* 118 (1988), 139–76, ibid., 177–79; M.C. Bishop (ed.), *Roman Inveresk: Past, Present and Future* (Duns, 2002)

Kirkland (NX 804901) *Britannia* 21 (1990) 312; 24 (1993), 281

Ladyward (NY 113820) *Britannia* 21 (1990), 313

Lamington (NS 977309) RCAHMS, *Lanarkshire*, 160

Lantonside (NY 010662) *Britannia* 16 (1985), 267

Linlithgow (NT 001773) RCAHMS, *Midlothian and West Lothian*, 219

Little Clyde (NS 994159) RCAHMS, *Lanarkshire*, 134–35

Livingston (NT 039666) *Britannia* 24 (1993), 280

Loudoun Hill (NS 605371) S.N. Miller, *ROSWS*, 188–91; D.L. Kennedy, *Britannia* 7 (1976), 286–87

Luce Sands (NX 141556) D.J. Breeze and J.N.G. Ritchie, *TDGNHAS* 55 (1979), 77–85

Lurg Moor (NS 295738) *JRS* 43 (1953), 105; A.S. Robertson, *PSAS* 97 (1963–64), 198–200

Lyne (NT 187405) K.A. Steer and R.W. Feachem, *PSAS* 95 (1961–62), 208–18; RCAHMS, *Peeblesshire*, 171–75

Milton (NT 092014) J. Clarke, *TDGNHAS* 28 (1949–50), 199–221

Mollins (NS 713718) W.S. Hanson and G.S. Maxwell, *Britannia* 11 (1980), 43–49

Newstead (NT 571343) J. Curle, *A Roman Frontier Post and its People: the Fort of Newstead* (Glasgow, 1911); RCAHMS, *Roxburghshire*, 312–20; E. W. Black, *PSAS* 121 (1991), 215–22; W. Elliot, *The Trimontium Story* (Melrose, 1998); S. Clarke and A. Wise, *PSAS* 129 (1999), 373–91; J.W. Elliot and M. Henig, *PSAS* 129 (1999), 393–98; S. Clarke, *PSAS* 130 (2000), 457–67; frequent reports in *DES* and *Britannia*.

North Slipperfield (NT 130520) *Britannia* 27 (1996), 404

Oakwood (NT 425249) K.A. Steer and R.W. Feachem, *PSAS* 86 (1951–52), 81–105; RCAHMS, *Selkirkshire*, 99–102

Outerwards (NS 232666) F. Newall, *GAJ* 4 (1976), 111–23

Oxton (NT 491546) J.K. St Joseph, *JRS* 48 (1958), 88; G.S. Maxwell and D.R. Wilson, *Britannia* 18 (1987), 25

Pathhead (NT 397636) J.K. St Joseph, *JRS* 48 (1958), 88; *Britannia* 29 (1998), 380

Pennymuir (NT 755140) RCAHMS, *Roxburghshire*, 375–77

Raeburnfoot (NY 251990) A.S. Robertson, *TDGNHAS* 29 (1960–61), 24–29

Redshaw Burn (NT 030139) S.N. Miller, *ROSWS*, 111; RCAHMS, *Lanarkshire*, 134–35

Rubers Law (NT 580156) RCAHMS, *Roxburghshire*, 102–5; L. Keppie, *GAJ* 16 (1989–90), 5

Sanquhar (NS 785106) *Britannia* 16 (1985), 267

Tocherknowe (NT 141526) *Britannia* 24 (1993), 283

Torwood (NY 122819) S.N. Miller, *ROSWS*, 101

Traprain Law (NT 580747), A.O. Curle, *The Traprain Treasure* (Glasgow, 1923); G. Jobey, in D.W. Harding (ed.), *Hillforts: Later Prehistoric Earthworks in Britan and Ireland* (London, 1976), 191–204; M.F. Sekulla, *PSAS* 112 (1982), 285–94; M. Erdrich, K.M. Giannotta and W.S. Hanson, *PSAS* 130 (2000), 441–56

Wandel (NS 944268) RCAHMS, *Lanarkshire*, 136

Ward Law (NY 024668) S. N. Miller, *ROSWS*, 117–20; A. Truckell, *TDGNHAS* 27 (1948–49), 203; G.S. Maxwell and D.R. Wilson, *Britannia* 18 (1987), 23f

White Type (NT 055119) S.N. Miller, *ROSWS*, 24

Woden Law (NT 767125) RCAHMS, *Roxburghshire*, 169–72; I.A. Richmond and J. K. St Joseph, *PSAS* 112 (1982), 277–84

The Antonine Wall

General: G.B. Bailey, 'The provision of fort-annexes on the Antonine Wall', *PSAS* 124 (1994), 299–314; idem, 'Stream crossings on the Antonine Wall', *PSAS* 126 (1996), 347–69; idem, *The Antonine Wall: Rome's Northern Frontier* (Falkirk, 2003); G.B. Bailey and D.F. Devereux, 'The eastern terminus of the Antonine Wall: a review', *PSAS* 117 (1987), 93–104; W.S. Hanson and G.S. Maxwell,

Rome's North-West Frontier: the Antonine Wall (Edinburgh, 1983); G. Macdonald, *The Roman Wall in Scotland* (Glasgow, 1911; 2nd ed., Oxford, 1934); A.S. Robertson, *The Antonine Wall* (Glasgow, 1960; 5th ed., revised by L. Keppie, Glasgow, 2001); D. Skinner, *The Countryside of the Antonine Wall* (Perth, 1973); K.A. Steer, 'The Nature and Purpose of the Expansions on the Antonine Wall', *PSAS* 90 (1956–57), 161–69; V.G. Swan, 'The Twentieth Legion and the history of the Antonine Wall reconsidered', *PSAS* 129 (1999), 399–480; D.J. Woolliscroft, 'Signalling and the design of the Antonine Wall', *Britannia* 27 (1996), 153–77; RCAHMS, Inventories: *Stirlingshire* (Edinburgh, 1963); *Lanarkshire* (Edinburgh, 1978).

Auchendavy (NS 677749) L.J.F. Keppie and J.J. Walker, *Britannia* 16 (1985), 29–35; *Britannia* 31 (2000), 385; 33 (2002), 287.

Balmuildy (NS 581716) S.N. Miller, *The Roman Fort at Balmuildy* (Glasgow, 1922); *Britannia* 31 (2000), 383

Bar Hill (NS 707759) G. Macdonald and A. Park, *The Roman Forts on the Bar Hill* (Glasgow, 1906); A. Robertson, M. Scott and L.J.F. Keppie, *Bar Hill, a Roman Fort and its Finds* (Oxford, 1975); L.J.F. Keppie, *GAJ* 12 (1985), 49–81; idem, *SAJ* 24.1 (2002), 21–48

Bearsden (NS 545720) D.J. Breeze, 'The Roman Fort on the Antonine Wall at Bearsden', in D.J. Breeze (ed.), *Studies in Scottish Antiquity* (Edinburgh, 1984), 32–68; idem, *The Roman Fort at Bearsden*, forthcoming

Buchley enclosure (NS 595720) W.S. Hanson and G.S. Maxwell, *Britannia* 14 (1983), 227–43

Cadder (NS 616725) J. Clarke, *The Roman Fort at Cadder* (Glasgow, 1933)

Carriden (NT 025807) J.K. St Joseph, *PSAS* 83 (1948–49), 167–74; I.A. Richmond and K.A. Steer, *PSAS* 90 (1956–57), 1–7; A.J. Dunwell, *PSAS* 125 (1995), 602–6; *Britannia* 26 (1995), 332; G.B. Bailey, *PSAS* 127 (1997), 577–94

Castlecary (NS 790783) D. Christison and M. Buchanan, *PSAS* 37 (1902–3), 271–346; RCAHMS, *Stirlingshire*, 103–6

Castlehill (NS 525727) L.J.F. Keppie, *GAJ* 7 (1980), 80–84; *Britannia* 34 (2003), 304

Cleddans (NS 508723) L.J.F. Keppie and J.J. Walker, *Britannia* 12 (1981), 143–62

Croy Hill (NS 733765) G. Macdonald, *PSAS* 59 (1924–25), 288–90; ibid. 66 (1931–32), 243–76; ibid. 71 (1936–37), 32–71; W.S. Hanson and L.J.F. Keppie, *Current Archaeology* 62 (June 1978), 91–94;

W.S. Hanson, in J. Fitz (ed.), *Limes: Akten des XI internationalen Limeskongresses* (Budapest, 1977), 1–9

Dullatur camps (NS 746767) C.E. Lowe and R. Moloney, *Britannia* 31 (2000), 239–53

Duntocher (NS 495726) A.S. Robertson, *An Antonine Fort, Golden Hill, Duntocher* (Edinburgh and London 1957); V.G. Swan, *PSAS* 129 (1999), 431–33; L.J.F. Keppie, *Britannia* 35 (2004), 179–224

Falkirk (NS 886798) RCAHMS, *Stirlingshire*, 99; D.J. Breeze, *PSAS* 106 (1974–75), 200–3; L.J.F. Keppie and J.F. Murray, *PSAS* 111 (1981), 248–62; G.B. Bailey, *Calatria* 1 (1991), 5–17; idem, *PSAS* 125 (1995), 577–600

Garnhall camps (NS 780779 and 785780) L.J.F. Keppie and K. Speller, *PSAS* 125 (1995), 631–43; *Britannia* 24 (1993), 279; 25 (1994), 225; 26 (1995), 334; 27 (1996), 400; A.S. Robertson, *The Antonine Wall* (Glasgow, 2001), 79

Glasgow Bridge (NS 636731) RCAHMS, *Lanarkshire*, 134

Inveravon (NS 951796) A.S. Robertson, *GAJ* 1 (1969), 37–42; A. Dunwell and I. Ralston, *PSAS* 125 (1995), 521–76

Kinneil (NS 977803) L.J.F. Keppie and J.J. Walker, *Britannia* 12 (1981), 143–62; G.B.Bailey and J. Cannel, *PSAS* 126 (1996), 303–46; B. Glendinning, *PSAS* 130 (2000), 509–24

Kirkintilloch (NS 651739) A.S. Robertson, *PSAS* 97 (1963–64), 180–88; J.H. McBrien, *PSAS* 125 (1995), 650–56; *Britannia* 26 (1995), 336

Mumrills (NS 918794) G. Macdonald and A.O. Curle, *PSAS* 63 (1928–29), 396–575; K.A. Steer, *PSAS* 94 (1960–61), 86–132; RCAHMS, *Stirlingshire*, 96–99; frequent reports in *DES* and *Britannia*

Old Kilpatrick (NS 460731) S.N. Miller, *The Roman Fort at Old Kilpatrick* (Glasgow 1928); L.J.F. Keppie, *PSAS* 125 (1995), 658–59; A. Leslie, R.P.J. McCullagh, K. Speller, *PSAS* 132 (2002), 293–96

Rough Castle (NS 843798) M. Buchanan, D. Christison, J. Anderson, *PSAS* 39 (1904–5), 442–99; RCAHMS, *Stirlingshire*, 102; I. MacIvor, M.C. Thomas and D.J. Breeze, *PSAS* 110 (1978–80), 230–85; I. Máté, *PSAS* 125 (1995), 483–97

Seabegs Wood (NS 812792) L.J.F. Keppie and J.J. Walker, *Britannia* 12 (1981), 143–62

Summerston (NS 578722) *Britannia* 12 (1981), 320

Watling Lodge (NS 862797) D.J. Breeze, *PSAS* 105 (1972–74), 166–75; G.B. Bailey, *PSAS* 125 (1995), 622–26, 664

Westerwood (NS 760773) G. Macdonald, *PSAS* 67 (1932–33), 243–96;

L.J.F. Keppie, *GAJ* 5 (1979), 9–18; idem, *GAJ* 19 (1994–95), 83–99
Wilderness Plantation (NS 597721) J.J. Wilkes, *GAJ* 3 (1974), 51–65;
   RCAHMS, *Lanarkshire*, 136–7

Scotland North of the Antonine Wall

General (including roads): O.G.S. Crawford, *Topography of Roman
   Scotland North of the Antonine Wall* (hereafter *TRSNAW*)
   (Cambridge, 1949); RCAHMS, Inventory: *Stirlingshire* (Edinburgh,
   1963); RCAHMS, *South-East Perth: an Archaeological Landscape*
   (Edinburgh, 1994)
Abernethy (NO 174165) J.K. St Joseph, *JRS* 63 (1973), 219–20
Ardoch (NN 839099) D. Christison, J.H. Cunningham, J. Anderson,
   T. Ross, *PSAS* 32 (1897–98), 399–476; J.K. St Joseph, *Britannia* 1
   (1970), 163–78; idem, *JRS* 67 (1977), 135–38; D.J. Breeze, *PSAS* 102
   (1969–1970), 122–28; idem, in A. O'Connor and D.V. Clarke (eds.),
   From the Stone Age to the 'Forty-five (Edinburgh 1983), 224–36; D.J.
   Breeze, *Ardoch Roman Fort, Braco, near Dunblane: a Guide* (Bridge of
   Allan, 1983; new. ed., 1987); *Britannia* 26 (1995), 332; 28 (1997), 405
Arthur's O'on (NS 879827) K.A. Steer, *Arch. J.* 115 (1958), 99–110;
   RCAHMS, Stirlingshire, 118; I.G. Brown, *Antiquity* 48 (1974), 283–
   87
Auchinhove (NJ 463517) J.K. St Joseph, *JRS* 63 (1973), 227–28
Balmakewan (NO 665666) J.K. St Joseph, *JRS* 59 (1969), 112
Bellie (NJ 355613) O.G.S. Crawford, *TRSNAW*, 122–25; J.K. St Joseph,
   JRS 59 (1969), 113–14
Bertha (NO 097268) O.G.S. Crawford, *TRSNAW*, 56–62; H.C.
   Adamson and D.B. Gallagher, *PSAS* 116 (1986), 195–204
Black Hill (NO 176391) I.A. Richmond, *PSAS* 74 (1939–40), 37–40
Blackhill Wood, Ardoch (NN 845108), B.D. Glendinning and A.J.
   Dunwell, *Britannia* 31 (2000), 255–90
Bochastle (NN 614079) W.A. Anderson, *TGAS* n.s. 14 (1956), 35–63;
   J.K. St Joseph, *JRS* 63 (1973), 224
Buchlyvie (NS 586943) L. Main, *PSAS* 128 (1998), 293–417
Burnfield (NJ 540476) *Britannia* 15 (1984), 273
Caddam Wood, Kirriemuir (NO 391556); O.G.S. Crawford, *TRSNAW*,
   91ff
Camelon (NS 863809) D. Christison, M. Buchanan, J. Anderson,

PSAS 35 (1900–01), 329–417; RCAHMS, *Stirlingshire*, 107–12; D.J. Breeze, J. Close-Brooks and J.N.G. Ritchie, *Britannia* 7 (1976), 73–95; N. McCord and J. Tait, *PSAS* 109 (1977–78), 151–65; T.W.T. Tatton-Brown, *Britannia* 11 (1980), 340–43; V.A. Maxfield, *Scottish Archaeological Forum* 12 (1980), 69–78; V.G. Swan and P.T. Bidwell, in J. Bird (ed.), *Form and Fabric: Studies in Rome's material Past in Honour of B.R. Hartley* (Oxford, 1998), 21–30; *Britannia* 30 (1999), 328; G.B. Bailey, *PSAS* 130 (2000), 469–89

Cardean (NO 289460) A.S. Robertson, in D. Haupt and H.G. Horn (eds), *Studien zu den Militärgrenzen Roms* II (Köln/Bonn 1977), 65–74; *Britannia* 33 (2002), 285

Cargill (NO 163376 and NO 166379) I.A. Richmond, *JRS* 33 (1943), 47; G.S. Maxwell and D.R. Wilson, *Britannia* 18 (1987), 16

Carpow (NO 208179) R.E. Birley, *PSAS* 96 (1962–63), 184–207; J.K. St Joseph, *JRS* 63 (1973), 220–23; R.P. Wright, *Britannia* 5 (1974), 289–92; J.N. Dore and J.J. Wilkes, *PSAS* 129 (1999), 481–575

Cleaven Dyke (NO 156408-171399) I.A. Richmond, *PSAS* 74 (1939–40), 37–38; H.C. Adamson and D.B. Gallagher, *GAJ* 13 (1986), 63–68; G.J. Barclay, G.S. Maxwell, I.A. Simpson and D.A. Davidson, *Antiquity* 69 (1995), 317–26; G.J. Barclay and G.S. Maxwell, *The Cleaven Dyke and Littleour: Monuments in the Neolithic of Tayside* (Edinburgh, 1998)

Dalginross (NN 773210) O.G.S. Crawford, *TRSNAW*, 41–44; A.S. Robertson, *PSAS* 97 (1963–64), 196–98; J.K. St Joseph, *JRS* 59 (1969), 109; I.M. Rogers, *PSAS* 123 (1993), 277–90; *Britannia* 31 (2000), 381

Doune (NN 727012) G.S. Maxwell, *Britannia* 15 (1984), 217–23; G.S. Maxwell and D.R. Wilson, *Britannia* 18 (1987), 17; *Britannia* 31 (2000), 381

Drumquhassle (NS 484874) G.S. Maxwell, *Britannia* 14 (1983), 167–81; G.S. Maxwell and D.R. Wilson, *Britannia* 18 (1987), 17; *Britannia* 30 (1999), 328; 31 (2000), 381

Dunipace (NS 841821) *Britannia* 15 (1984), 275; 20 (1989), 271; 21 (1990), 230

Dunning (NO 025148) J.K. St Joseph, *JRS* 63 (1973), 218–19; A.J. Dunwell and L.J.F. Keppie, *Britannia* 26 (1995), 51–62

Durno (NJ 699272) J.K. St Joseph, *Britannia* 9 (1978), 271–88

Easter Galcantray (NH 810483), R.A. Gregory, *PSAS* 131 (2001), 177–222

Fendoch (NN 919283) I.A. Richmond and J. McIntyre, *PSAS* 73 (1938–39), 110–54

Gask Ridge (NN 917185 to NO 075-245) D. Christison, *PSAS* 35 (1900–1), 15–43; A.S. Robertson, in *Trans. Perthshire Soc. of Natural Sciences* 1974, 14–29; D.J. Woolliscroft, *PSAS* 123 (1993), 291–313; idem, *PSAS* 130 (2000), 491–507; idem, *The Roman Frontier on the Gask Ridge, Perth and Kinross* (BAR Brit. ser. 335, Oxford, 2002)

Glenbank (NN 812057) G.S. Maxwell, *DES* 1984, 4; *Britannia* 31 (2000), 379

Glenmailen (NJ 655381) G. Macdonald *PSAS* 50 (1915-16), 348–59; J.K. St Joseph, *Britannia* 1 (1970), 163–78; idem, *JRS* 63 (1973), 226

Gourdie (NO 115427) I.A. Richmond, *JRS* 33 (1943), 47; O.G.S. Crawford, *TRSNAW*, 75–76

Grassy Walls (NO 105280) O.G.S. Crawford, *TRSNAW*, 64–67; J.K. St Joseph, *JRS* 48 (1958), 91

Greenloaning (NN 831072) D.J. Woolliscroft and B. Hoffmann, *PSAS* 127 (1997), 563–76

Inchtuthil (NO 125397) J. Abercromby, T. Ross, J. Anderson, *PSAS* 36 (1901–2), 182–242; L. Pitts and J.K. St Joseph, *Inchtuthil, the Roman Legionary Fortress* (London, 1985); E.A.M. Shirley, *The Construction of the Roman Legionary Fortress at Inchtuthil* (BAR Brit. ser. 298, Oxford, 2000)

Innerpeffray (NN 916182 and 907182) J.K. St Joseph, *JRS* 48 (1958), 90; ibid. 59 (1969), 116

Inverquharity (NO 405582) G.S. Maxwell and D.R. Wilson, *Britannia* 18 (1987), 15–16; *Britannia* 34 (2003), 300

Kaims Castle (NN 860129) D. Christison, *PSAS* 35 (1900–01), 1543

Kair House (NO 767765) J.K. St Joseph, *JRS* 55 (1965), 83; (1973), 233

Kintore (NJ 787162) O.G.S. Crawford, *TRSNAW*, 112–15; J.K. St Joseph, *JRS* 67 (1977), 140; A.N. Shepherd, *PSAS* 116 (1986), 205–09; *Britannia* 33 (2002), 285; 34 (2003), 300

Kirkbuddo (NO 491442) O.G.S. Crawford, *TRSNAW*, 97–100; J.K. St Joseph, *JRS* 48 (1958), 92–94; 55 (1965), 83

Leckie broch (NS 692940) E.W. MacKie, *GAJ* 9 (1982), 60–72; ibid., 14 (1987), 1–18

Lintrose (NO 220376) O.G.S. Crawford, *TRSNAW*, 84–86; J.K. St Joseph, *JRS* 45 (1955), 87

Malling (NN 564000) J.K. St Joseph, *JRS* 63 (1973), 223–24

Muiryfold (NJ 489520) J.K. St Joseph, *JRS* 51 (1961), 123; 59 (1969), 118

Normandykes (NO 829993) O.G.S. Crawford, *TRSNAW*, 110–12

Raedykes (NO 841902) G. Macdonald, *PSAS* 50 (1915–16), 317–48; J.K. St Joseph, *JRS* 59 (1969), 118

Scone (NO 104270) J.K. St Joseph, *JRS* 48 (1958), 92–94; 55 (1965), 83

Shielhill North (NN 856122) D.J. Woolliscroft, *The Roman Frontier on the Gask Ridge* (Oxford, 2002), 68–76

Shielhill South (NN 850115) D.J. Woolliscroft and B. Hoffmann, *PSAS* 128 (1998), 441–60

Sma' Glen (NN 908284) RCAHMS records

Stracathro (NO 617657) J.K. St Joseph, *Britannia* 1 (1970), 163–78; A.S. Robertson, in D. Haupt and H.G. Horn (eds), *Studien zu den Militärgrenzen Roms* II (Köln/Bonn, 1977), 65–74

Strageath (NN 898180) O.G.S. Crawford, *TRSNAW*, 40–41; S.S. Frere and J.J. Wilkes, *Strageath: Excavations within the Roman Fort, 1973–86* (London, 1989)

Westerton (NN 873146) W.S. Hanson and J.G.P. Friel, *PSAS* 125 (1995), 499–519

INDEX

BIRLINN LTD (incorporating John Donald and Polygon) is one of Scotland's leading publishers with over four hundred titles in print. Should you wish to be put on our catalogue mailing list **contact**:

Catalogue Request
Birlinn Ltd
West Newington House
10 Newington Road
Edinburgh EH9 1QS
Scotland, UK

Tel: + 44 (0) 131 668 4371
Fax: + 44 (0) 131 668 4466
e-mail: info@birlinn.co.uk

Postage and packing is free within the UK. For overseas orders, postage and packing (airmail) will be charged at 30% of the total order value.

For more information, or to order online, visit our website at **www.birlinn.co.uk**